. 1

A gift from
the Rev. Canon James Daughtry
in 1995
to the Holy Faith Library

His Life Is Mine

BY

ARCHIMANDRITE SOPHRONY

Translated from the Russian by Rosemary Edmonds

ST. VLADIMIR'S SEMINARY PRESS

Crestwood, New York 10707

1977

First published 1977
by A. R. Mowbray & Co Ltd
The Alden Press, Osney Mead
Oxford OX₂ OEG

This American edition published by special arrangement with A. R. Mowbray
& Co. Limited and St. Vladimir's Seminary Press.

Library of Congress Cataloging in Publication Data

Sofronii, Archimandrite, 1896—
    His life is mine.
    1. Christian life—Orthodox Eastern authors. 2. Prayer.
3. Jesus prayer. I. Title.
BX382.S6313   248'.48'193   76—56815
ISBN 0-913836-33-8

Also by Archimandrite Sophrony:

WISDOM FROM MOUNT ATHOS
St. Vladimir's Seminary Press, 1975

THE MONK OF MOUNT ATHOS
St. Vladimir's Seminary Press, 1975

PHOTOLITHOPRINTED BY EERDMANS PRINTING COMPANY
GRAND RAPIDS, MICHIGAN, UNITED STATES OF AMERICA

Contents

Introduction

Archimandrite Sophrony was born in 1896, to Orthodox parents in Tsarist Russia. From childhood he showed a rare capacity for prayer and as a young boy would ponder questions heavy with centuries of theological debate. A sense of exile in this world spoke of an infinite always embracing our finitude. Prayer entails the idea of eternity with God. In prayer the reality of the living God is yoked with the concrete reality of earthly life. If we know what a man reverences, we know the most important thing about him—what it is that determines his character and behaviour. The author of *His Life is Mine* was early possessed by an urgent longing to penetrate to the heart of divine eternity through contemplation of the visible world. This craving, like a flame in the heart, irradiated his student days at the State School of Fine Arts in Moscow. This was the period when a parallel speculative interest in Buddhism and the whole arena of Indian culture changed the clef of his inner life. Eastern mysticism now seemed to him more profound than Christianity, the concept of a supra-personal Absolute more convincing than that of a Personal God. The Eastern mystics' notion of Being imparted overwhelming majesty to the transcendental. With the advent of the First World War and the subsequent Revolution in Russia he began to think of existence itself as the *causa causens* of all suffering and so strove, through meditation, to divest himself of all visual and mental images.

His studio was at the top of a tall house in a quiet part of Moscow. There he would labour for hours on end, straining every nerve to depict his subject dispassionately, to convey its temporal significance, yet at the same time to use it as a spring-board for exploring the infinite. He was tortured by conflicting arguments:

if life was generated by the eternal, why did his body need to breathe, eat, sleep, and so on? Why did it react to every variation in the physical atmosphere? In an effort to break out of the narrow framework of existence he took up yoga and applied himself to meditation. But he never lost his keen awareness of the beauty of nature.

Daily life now flowed on the periphery, as it were, of external events. The one thing needful was to discover the purport of our appearance on this planet; to revert to the moment before creation and be merged with our original source. He continued oblivious to social and political affairs—utterly preoccupied by the thought that if man dies without the possibility of returning to the sphere of Absolute Being, then life held no meaning. Occasionally, meditation would bring respite with an illusion of some unending quietude which had been his fountain-head.

The turmoil of the post-Revolutionary period made it increasingly difficult for artists to work in Russia, and in 1921 the author started to search for ways and means of emigrating to Europe—to France, in particular, as the centre of the world for painters. *En route* he managed to travel through Italy, looking long at the great masterpieces of the Renaissance. After a brief stay in Berlin he finally reached Paris and flung head, heart and soul into painting. His career made a satisfactory start: the Salon d'Automne accepted his first canvas and the Salon des Tuileries, the élite of the Salon d'Automne, invited him to exhibit with them. But on another level all was not going as he had expected. Art began to lose its significance as a means to liberation and immortality for the spirit. Even lasting fame would be but a ludicrous caricature of genuine immortality. The finest artefact is worthless when considered against the background of infinity.

Little by little it dawned on him that pure intellection, an activity of the brain only, could not advance one far in the search for reality. Then suddenly he remembered Christ's injunction to love God 'with all thy *heart*, and with all thy mind'. This unexpected insight was as portentous as that earlier moment when the Eastern vision of a supra-personal Being had beguiled him into dismissing the Gospel message as a call to the emotions. Only that

8

earlier moment had struck dark as a thunderclap, while now revelation illuminated like lightning. Intellection without love was not enough. Actual knowledge could only come through community of being, which meant love. And so Christ conquered: His teaching appealed to his mind with different undertones, acquired other dimensions. Prayer to the Personal God was restored to his heart—directed, first and foremost, to Christ.

He must decide on a new way of living. He enrolled in the then recently opened Paris Orthodox Theological Institute, in the hope of being taught how to pray, and the right attitude towards God; how to overcome one's passions and attain divine eternity. But formal theology produced no key to the kingdom of heaven. He left Paris and made his way to Mount Athos where men seek union with God through prayer. Setting foot on the Holy Mountain, he kissed the ground and besought God to accept and further him in this new life. Next, he looked for a mentor who would help extricate him from a series of apparently insoluble problems. He threw himself into prayer as fervently as he previously had in France. It was crystal-clear that if he really wanted to know God and be with Him entirely, he must dedicate himself to just that— and still more entirely than he had to painting in the old days. Prayer became both garment and breath to him, unceasing even when he slept. Despair combined with a feeling of resurrection in his soul: despair over the peoples of the earth who had forsaken God and were expiring in their ignorance. At times while praying for them he would be driven to wrestle with God as their Creator. This oscillation between the two extremes of hell on the one side and Divine Light on the other made it urgent that someone should spell out the point of what was happening to him. But another four years were to pass before the first encounter with the Staretz Silouan which he quickly recognised as the most precious gift Providence ever made to him. He would not have dared dream of such a miracle, though he had long hungered and thirsted after a counsellor who would hold out a strong hand and explain the laws of spiritual life. For eight years or so he sat at the feet of his Gamaliel, until the Staretz' death when he begged for the blessing of the Monastery Superior and Council to depart into the 'desert'. Soon after, the Second World War broke out, rumours of which (no actual news filtered through to the wilderness) intensified his prayer for all humanity. He would spend the night hours prone on the earth floor of his cave, imploring God to intervene in the crazy blood-bath. He prayed for those who were being killed, for those who were killing, for all in torment. And he prayed that God would not allow the more evil side to win.

During the war years the desert felt remarkably more silent and withdrawn than of wont, since the German occupation of Greece barred all traffic on the sea around the Athonite peninsula. But the author's total seclusion ended when he was urged to become confessor and spiritual father to the brethren of the Monastery of St Paul. Staretz Silouan had predicted that he would one day be a confessor and had exhorted him not to shrink from this crucial form of service to people—service which necessitates giving oneself to the supplicant, accepting him into one's own life, sharing with him one's deepest feelings. Before long he was called to other monasteries, and monks from the small hermitages of Athos, anchorites and solitaries turned to him. It was a difficult and heavily responsible mission but he reasoned to himself that it was his duty to try and repay the succour which he had received from his fathers in God, who had so lovingly shared with him the knowledge granted to them from on High. He could not keep their teaching to himself. He must give freely of what he had freely received. But to be a spiritual counsellor is no easy task: it involves transferring to others attention hitherto destined for oneself, looking with imaginative sympathy into other hearts and minds, contending with my neighbour's problems instead of my own.

After four years spent in a remote spot surrounded by mountain crags and rocks, with little water and almost no vegetation, the author assented to a suggestion from the Monastery of St Paul to move into a grotto on their land. This new cave had many advantages for an anchorite-priest. There were many hermits in the desert and they tended to settle close to one another, though hidden from sight by boulders and cliffs. Here, besides being completely isolated, there was a tiny chapel, some ten feet by seven, hewn out of the rock-face. But winter was a trying time. The first downpour would flood the previously dry cave and then every day for perhaps six months he was obliged to scoop up and throw outside some hundred buckets of water. He put up some iron sheeting to prevent the water soaking his couch. Only the little chapel stayed dry. There he could pray, and keep his books. Everywhere else was wet. Impossible to light a fire and warm up something to eat. In the end, after the third winter, failing health compelled him to abandon the grotto which had afforded the rare privilege of living detached from the world.

It was now that the idea came to him of writing a book about Staretz Silouan, to record the precepts which had so helped him to find his bearings in the wide expanses of the spirit by instructing him in the ways of spiritual combat. To carry out this project he would have to go back to the West—to France, where he had felt more at home than in any other country in Europe. His first intention was to stay for a year but then he found that he would need more time. Working in difficult conditions, he fell dangerously ill and a serious operation left him an invalid, causing him to lay aside all thought of returning to a desert cave on Mount Athos.

The preliminary edition of his book concerning Staretz Silouan he roneo-typed himself. A printed edition followed in 1952. Thereafter the translations began: first into English (*The Undistorted Image*), then German, Greek, French, Serbian, with excerpts in still other languages. The reaction of the ascetics of the Holy Mountain was of extreme importance to the author. They confirmed the book as a true reflection of the ancient traditions of Eastern monasticism, and recognised the Staretz as spiritual heir to the great Fathers of Egypt, Palestine, Sinai and other historic schools of asceticism dating back to the beginning of the Christian era.

Archimandrite Sophrony felt convinced that Christ's injunction, 'Keep thy mind in hell, and despair not', was directed through Staretz Silouan to our century especially, drowned as it is in despair. (Are not the 'perilous times' come, 'when men shall be lovers of their own selves . . . unthankful, unholy . . . trucebreakers, false accusers . . . despisers of those that are good . . . lovers of pleasures more than lovers of God; having a form of godliness but denying the power thereof . . . ever learning, and never able to come to knowledge of the truth'?) He believed, too, that as the Staretz had prayed for decades with such extraordinary love for the human race, entreating God to grant all mankind to know Him in the Holy Spirit, so men would love the Staretz in return. The Russian poet Pushkin claimed that no monument would be necessary to keep alive remembrance of him—his fellow countrymen would long cherish his memory for he had sung of freedom in a cruel age, of mercy to the fallen. Had not the Staretz in his humility rendered a still nobler service to humanity? He taught us how to drive away despair, explaining what lay at the back of this terrible spiritual state. He revealed to us the Living God and His love for the sons of Adam. He taught us how to interpret the Gospel in its eternal aspects. And for many he made the word of Christ real, part of everyday life. Above all, he restored to our souls a firm hope of blessed eternity in the Divine Light.

Throughout this book Archimandrite Sophrony reflects the teaching of his spiritual father. Not all of it will be intelligible at first perusal—in fact, it is not easy reading on any reckoning. Form must be sacrificed to content when the translator is caught in the uncomfortable limbo between languages; and in a work of this kind the author is so often speaking across a semantic chasm. Few of us have any inkling of the life described in these pages. But close study will make us familiar with the Athonite ascetic's manner of living, and then we can with profit try to apply some of the lessons learned to our own case. Grace, which is God's gift of holiness, depends upon man's attempt at holiness.

The author believes ardently in the perfectibility of man, and with loud and tidal words stokes our fires. He declares roundly, over and over again, that prayer is the surest way to true knowledge of God. God for him is presence, manifesting Himself in all things. We all possess a divine spark. Our freedom is in direct proportion to the degree of consciousness possessed by us. Only the Eternal can give meaning to life. The collapse of an absolute value leads to the collapse of relative values. When God collapses, so does honour, honesty, loyalty and the like. A culture, a civilisation can only be as strong as the inner lives of its people. The only revolution that we should be thinking about is a personal, private moral one.

Faithful in spirit to the charge laid upon him by his Staretz, some twenty years ago Archimandrite Sophrony founded a small community in Essex, where at first he would receive all who appealed to him for spiritual help. Now, however, age and declining strength have forced him to hand over much of his former activity to his monks, in order to devote his energy to the Liturgy. The hours celebrating the Liturgy give the day its sense and heart. He lives the Liturgy, not in abstract fashion but by commitment and loving in the very thick of human suffering. He is full to the brim with awareness of God. Often he gives the impression of a man in touch with unknown modes of being, who sees light deep in the silence. He is clear, merciful and severe in his judgments, which stimulate one to new insights. He has the hard and gentle eyes of an escetic. For him, creation is another word for hope. If a man possesses only what he gives away, the author of this book is blessed indeed.

R.E.

PART 1

I

Knowledge of God

O Thou Who art:
O God the Father, Almighty Master:
Who hast created us and brought us into this life:
Vouchsafe that we may know Thee,
The one true God.

The human spirit hungers for knowledge—for entire, integral knowledge. Nothing can destroy our longing to know and, naturally, our ultimate craving is for knowledge of Primordial Being, of Whom or What actually exists. All down the ages man has paid instinctive homage to this First Principle. Our fathers and forefathers reverenced Him in different ways because they did not know him 'as he is, (1 John 3.2). Some (surely they were among the wisest) set up 'an altar with this inscription, TO THE UN-KNOWN GOD' (Acts 17.23). Even in our day we are continually made aware that reason *per se* cannot advance us over the threshold to the 'Unknown'. God is our only means of access to this higher knowledge, if He will reveal Himself.

The problem of knowledge of God sends the mind searching back through the centuries for instances of God appearing to man through one or other of the prophets. There can be no doubt that for us, for the whole Christian world, one of the most important happenings recorded in the chronicles of time was God's manifestation on Mount Sinai where Moses received new knowledge of Divine Being: 'I AM THAT I AM' (Exos. 3.14)—Jehovah. From that moment vast horizons opened out before mankind, and history took a new turn. A people's spiritual condition is the real cause of historical events: it is not the visible that is of primary importance but the invisible, the spiritual. Perceptions and ideas concerning being, and the meaning of life generally, seek expression and in so doing instigate the historical event.

Moses, possessed of the supreme culture of Egypt, did not question that the revelation that he was so miraculously given came from Him Who had indeed created the whole universe. In the Name of this God, I AM, he persuaded the Jewish people to follow him. Invested with extraordinary power from Above, he performed many wonders. To Moses belongs the undying glory of having brought mankind nearer to Eternal Truth. Convinced of the authenticity of his vision, he issued his injunctions as prescripts from on High. All things were effected in the Name and by the Name of the I AM Who had revealed Himself. Mighty is this Name in its strength and holiness—it is action proceeding from God. This Name was the first ingress into the *living* eternity; the dayspring of knowledge of the unoriginate Absolute as I AM.

In the Name of Jehovah Moses led the still primitive Israelites out of their captivity in Egypt. During their wanderings in the desert, however, he discovered that his people were far from ready, despite the many miracles they had witnessed, to receive the sublime revelation of the Eternal. This became particularly clear as they approached the borders of the Promised Land. Their faintheartedness and lack of faith caused the Lord to declare that none of those impregnated with the spirit of Egypt should see the 'good land' (Deut. 1.32,35,38). They would leave their bones in the wilderness, and Moses would encourage and prepare a new generation more capable of apprehending God—Invisible but holding all things in the palm of His hand.

Moses was endowed with exceptional genius but we esteem him more especially because he realised that the revelation granted to him, for all its grandeur and validity, was not yet complete. He sensed that He Who had revealed Himself was the 'first and the last' (Is. 44.6); that there could be no one and nothing before Him or after Him. And he sang: 'Give ear, O ye heavens, and I will speak; and hear, O earth, the words of my mouth' (Deut. 32.1). At the same time he continued to pray for better knowledge of God, calling to Him out of the depths: 'Shew me Thyself [as

Thou art], that I may know thee' (Exos. 33.13; 1 John 3.2). God heard his prayer and revealed Himself in so far as Moses could apprehend, for Moses could not contain the whole revelation. 'I will make all my goodness pass before thee, and I will proclaim the name of the Lord before thee . . . [and] while my glory passeth by, I . . . will cover thee with my hand . . . And I will take away mine hand, and thou shalt see my back parts: but my face shall not be seen' (Exos. 33.19,22,23).

That the revelation received by Moses was incomplete is shown in his testimony to the people that 'the Lord thy God will raise up unto thee a Prophet from the midst of thee . . . unto him ye shall hearken'. Also: 'And the Lord said unto me . . . I will raise them up a Prophet from among their brethren, like unto thee, and will put my words in his mouth, and he shall speak unto them all that I shall command him' (Deut. 18.15,18). According to the Old Testament all Israel lived in expectation of the coming of the Prophet of whom 'Moses wrote' (John 5.46), the Prophet *par excellence*, 'THAT prophet' (John 1.21). The Jewish people looked for the coming of the Messiah who when he was come would tell them 'all things' (John 4.25). *Come and live among us, that we may know Thee*, was the constant cry of the ancient Hebrews. Hence the name 'Emmanuel, which being interpreted is, God with us' (Is. 7.14; Matt. 1.23).

So for us Christians the focal point of the universe and the ultimate meaning of the entire history of the world is the coming of Jesus Christ, Who did not repudiate the archetypes of the Old Testament but vindicated them, unfolding to us their real significance and bringing new dimensions to all things—infinite, eternal dimensions. Christ's new covenant announces the beginning of a fresh period in the history of mankind. Now the Divine sphere was reflected in the searchless grandeur of the love and humility of God, our Father. With the coming of Christ all was changed: the new revelation affected the destiny of the whole created world.

It was given to Moses to know that Absolute Primordial Being is not some general entity, some impersonal cosmic process or supra-personal, all-transcending 'Non-Being'. It was proved to him that this Being had a *personal* character and was a *living* and

19

life-giving God. Moses, however, did not receive a clear vision: he did not see God in light as the apostles saw Him on Mount Tabor—'Moses drew near unto the thick darkness where God was' (Exos. 20.21). This can be interpreted variously but the stress lies on the incognisable character of God, though in what sense and in what connection we cannot be certain. Was Moses concerned with the impossibility of knowing the Essence of the Divine Being? Did he think that if God is Person, then He cannot be eternally single in Himself, for how could there be eternal metaphysical solitude? Here was this God ready to lead them but lead them where and for what purpose? What sort of immortality did He offer? Having reached the frontier of the Promised Land, Moses died.

And so He appeared, He to Whom the world owed its creation; and with rare exceptions 'the world knew him not' (John 1.10). The event was immeasurably beyond the ordinary man's grasp. The first to recognise Him was John the Baptist, for which reason he was rightly termed the greatest 'among them that are born of women' and the last of the law and the prophets (cf. Matt. 11.9–13).

Moses, as a man, needed obvious tokens of the power and authority bestowed on him, if he were to impress the Israelites, still prone to idol-worship, and compel them to heed his teaching. But it is impossible for us Christians to read the first books of the Old Testament without being appalled. In the Name of Jehovah all those who resisted Moses suffered fearful retribution and often death. Mount Sinai 'burned with fire', and the people were brought 'unto blackness, and darkness, and tempest', to 'the sound of a trumpet, and the voice of words, which . . . they could not endure' (Heb. 12.18–20).

It is the opposite with Christ. He came in utter meekness, the poorest of the poor with nowhere to lay His head. He had no authority, neither in the State nor even in the Synagogue founded on revelation from on High. He did not fight those who spurned Him. And it has been given to us to identify Him as the Pantocrator precisely because He 'made himself of no reputation, and took upon him the form of a servant' (Phil. 2.7), submitting finally to duress and execution. As the Creator and true Master of all that exists, He had no need of force, no need to display the power to punish opposition. He came 'to save the world' (John 12.47), to tell us of the One True God. He discovered to us the Name of Father. He gave us the word which He Himself had received from the Father. He revealed God to us as Light in Whom is no darkness at all (*cf*. 1 John 1,5). He made known the most exquisite mystery of all, that God is a Hypostatic Being, yet not One Person but Three Persons in One: the Holy Trinity. He gave us baptism 'with the Holy Ghost, and with fire' (Matt. 3.11). In the light of this knowledge we now see the path to eternal perfection (*cf*. Matt. 5.48).

The world continues to flounder in the vicious circle of its material problems—economic, class, nationalistic and the like—because people refuse to follow Christ. We have no wish to become like Him in all things: to become His brethren and through Him the beloved children of the Father and the chosen habitation of the Holy Spirit. In God's pre-eternal Providence for man we are meant to participate in His Being—to be like unto Him in all things. By its very essence this design on God's part for us excludes the slightest possibility of compulsion or predestination. And we as Christians must never renounce our goal lest we lose the inspiration to storm the kingdom of heaven. Experience shows all too clearly that once we Christians start reducing the scope of the revelation given to us by Christ and the Holy Spirit, we gradually cease to be attracted by the Light made manifest to us. If we are to preserve our saving hope, we must be bold. Christ said: 'Be of good cheer; I have overcome the world' (John 16.33). He had overcome the world in this instance not so much as God but as Man for He did in truth become man.

Genuine Christian life is lived 'in spirit and in truth' (John 4.23), and so can be continued in all places and at all times since the divine commandments of Christ possess an absolute character. In other words, there are and can be no circumstances anywhere on earth which could make observance of the commandments impossible.

In its eternal essence Christian life is divine spirit and truth and therefore transcends all outward forms. But man comes into this world as *tabula rasa*, to 'grow, wax strong in spirit, be filled with wisdom' (*cf.* Luke 2.40), and so the necessity arises for some kind of organisation to discipline and co-ordinate the corporate life of human beings still far from perfect morally, intellectually and, more important, spiritually. Our fathers in the Church and the apostles who taught us to honour the true God were well aware that, though the life of the Divine Spirit excels all earthly institutions, this same Spirit still constructs for Himself a dwelling-place of a tangible nature to serve as a vessel for the preservation of His gifts. This habitation of the Holy Spirit is the Church, which through centuries of tempest and violence has watched over the precious treasure of Truth as revealed by God. (We need not be concerned at this point with zealots who value framework rather than content.) 'The Lord is that Spirit: and where the Spirit of the Lord is, there is liberty . . . Beholding . . . the glory of the Lord, we are changed into the same image from glory to glory. (2 Cor. 3.17–18)' The Church's function is to lead the faithful to the luminous sphere of Divine Being. The Church is the spiritual centre of our world, encompassing the whole history of man. Those who through long ascetic struggle to abide in the Gospel precepts have become conscious of their liberty as sons of God no longer feel impeded by formal traditions—they can take general customs and ordinances in their stride. They have the example of Christ Who kept His Father's commandments without transgressing the law of Moses with all its 'burdens grievous to be borne' (Luke 11.46).

In Christ and the coming of the Holy Spirit God gave us the full and final revelation of Himself. His Being now for us is the First Reality, incomparably more evident than all the transient phenomena of this world. We sense His divine presence both within us and without: in the supreme majesty of the universe, in the human face, in the lightning flash of thought. He opens our eyes that we may behold and delight in the beauty of His creation. He fills our souls with love towards all mankind. His indescribably gentle touch pierces our heart. And in the hours when His imperishable Light illumines our heart we know that we shall not die. We know this with a knowledge impossible to prove in the ordinary way but which for us requires no proof, since the Spirit Himself bears witness within us.

The revelation of God as I AM THAT I AM proclaims the *personal* character of the Absolute God which is the core of His life. To interpret this revelation the Fathers adopted the philosophical term *hypostasis*, which first and foremost conveys actuality and can be applied to things, to man or to God. In many instances it was used as a synonym for *essence*. (*Substance* is the exact Latin translation.) In the Second Epistle to the Corinthians (2 Cor. 11.17) *hypostasis* denotes sober reality and is translated into English as *confidence* or *assurance*. In the Epistle to the Hebrews the term describes the Person of the Father: 'Who being . . . the express image of his person' (Heb. 1.3). Other renderings to be found in the same Epistle are *substance*—'Now faith is the substance of things hoped for' (Heb. 2.1)—and *very being*—'the stamp of God's very being' (N.E.B. Heb. 1.3). So then, these three words, *Person, substance, very being*, taken together impart the content of the Greek theological expression *hypostasis*, to be understood as comprising, on the one hand, the notion of *Countenance, Person*, while, on the other, stressing the cardinal importance of the personal dimension in Being. In the present text the terms *Hypostasis* and *Person(a)* are identical in meaning.

2

The Enigma of I AM

Primordial Being was made known to us in the Name I AM
THAT I AM (Exos. 3.13-14). Whoever has been blessed by a
vital encounter with Him is in some measure enabled to evaluate
the manifestations of God which the Old and New Testaments
describe. These progressive revelations of the heavenly spheres
are of paramount importance, besides which every other happening in world history pales into insignificance. Not only our secular
activity but all that the mind apprehends of the infinite cosmos
is a preparation for the unutterable miracle of the spirit's entry
into living Eternity compact of love.

Centuries passed before the true content of this amazing I AM
was understood. For all the fervour of their faith neither Moses
nor the prophets who were his heirs appreciated to the full the
blessing bestowed on them. They experienced God mainly
through historical events. If they turned to Him in spirit, they
contemplated in darkness. When we, sons of the New Testament,
read the Old Testament we notice how God tried to suggest to
our precursors that this I AM is One Being and at the same time
Three Persons. On occasions He would even speak of Himself as
We. 'And God said, Let *us* make man in *our* image, after *our*
likeness' (Gen. 1.26). 'And the Lord God said, Behold, man is
become as one of *us*' (Gen. 3.22). An even more remarkable
instance occurs with Abraham: three men appeared to him yet he
addressed them as if they were but one (*cf.* Gen. 18.2 *et seq.*).

The acquisition of knowledge of God is a slow process, not to
be achieved in all its plenitude from the outset, though God is
always and in His every manifestation invariably One and indivisible. Christ used simple language intelligible to the most

ignorant but what He said was above the heads even of the wisest of His listeners. 'Before Abraham was, I am' (John 8.58). 'I and my Father are one' (John 10.30). 'My Father will love him, and we will come unto him, and make our abode with him' (John 14.23). 'I will pray the Father, and he shall give you another Comforter, that he may abide with you for ever' (John 14.16). (So now a Third Person is introduced.) 'The Spirit of truth, which proceedeth from the Father, he shall testify of me' (John 15.26).

We note that Christ only gradually began to speak of the Father, and it was not until towards the close of His earthly life that He spoke of the Holy Spirit. Right to the end the disciples failed to understand Him, and He made no attempt to explain to them the image of Divine Being. 'I have yet many things to say unto you, but ye cannot bear them now' (John 16.12). Instead, He indicated how we might attain perfect knowledge: 'If ye continue in my word . . . ye shall know the truth' (John 8.31–32). 'The Holy Ghost . . . shall teach you all things, and bring all things to your remembrance, whatsoever I have said unto you' (John 14.26). 'When he the Spirit of truth, is come, he will guide you into all truth' (John 16.13). And He came, and revealed to us the fulness of Divine love but the gift was too much for our comprehension. Yet He does not withdraw but waits patiently for us to love Him, Christ, 'the power of God, and the wisdom of God' (1 Cor. 1.24), even as He loves us.

'The words that I speak unto you, they are spirit, and they are life' (John 6.63). It is just this life that we would consider now— life generated by prayer inspired from Above, through love coming down to us, and reasonable knowledge of Primordial Being.

How can one describe the state of the spirit to whom God is revealed as I AM? His closeness to one's heart is so tangible that joy in Him is like light. He is kind and gentle, and I can speak to Him intimately, face to Face, address Him—'Thou Who art'. And at the same time I realise that this I AM and this THOU WHO ART is all Being. He is unoriginate; self-existent; self-sufficient.

He is Person in the absolute sense. His consciousness penetrates all that exists. 'There is nothing covered, that shall not be revealed; and hid, that shall not be known . . . Are not two sparrows sold for a farthing? and one of them shall not fall on the ground without your Father. But the very hairs of your head are all numbered' (Matt. 10.26,29–30). 'Neither is there any creature that is not manifest in his sight: but all things are naked and opened unto the eyes of him with whom we have to do' (Heb. 4.13). Every moment of our life, our every heart-beat, is in His Hands. He is in truth the 'Light in which is no darkness at all' (1 John 1.5). And there is no one and nothing that can escape His all-seeing eye.

I AM THAT I AM. Yes, indeed, it is He Who is Being. He alone truly lives. Everything summoned from the abyss of non-being exists solely by His will. My individual life, down to the smallest detail, comes uniquely from Him. He fills the soul, binding her ever more intimately to Himself. Conscious contact with Him stamps a man for ever. Such a man will not now depart from the God of love Whom he has come to know. His mind is reborn. Hitherto he was inclined to see everywhere determined natural processes; now he begins to apprehend all things in the light of Person. Knowledge of the Personal God bears an intrinsically personal character. Like recognises like. There is an end to the deadly tedium of the impersonal. The earth, the whole universe, proclaims Him: 'heaven and earth praise him, the sea, and everything that moveth therein' (Ps. 69.34). And lo, He Himself seeks to be with us, to impart to us the abundance of His life (cf. John 10.10). And we for our part thirst for this gift.

The soul knows but cannot contain Him, and therein lies her pain. Our days are filled with longing to penetrate into the Divine sphere with every fibre of our being. Our prayer must be ardent, and many-sided is the experience that may be given. In our hearts, subjectively, it would seem—to judge by the love whose touch we feel—that the experience cannot be open to doubt. But despite the all-embracing surge of this love, despite the light in which it appears, it would not only be wrong but dangerous to rely exclusively on it. From Sacred Writ we know that the most pure Virgin Mary hurried off to her cousin Elisabeth to hear from her lips whether the revelation was true that she had received—of a son to be born to her who should be great and should be called the Son of God the Highest; and whose kingdom should have no end (*cf.* Luke 1.32–33). St Paul, who 'was caught up into paradise, and heard unspeakable words' (*cf.* 2 Cor. 12.4), affords another example. 'It pleased God . . . to reveal His Son in me'(Gal. 1.16); nevertheless, he went twice to Jerusalem to submit to Peter and others 'which were of reputation' (Gal. 2.1–2) the gospel he was preaching 'lest by any means [he] should run, or had run in vain' (Gal. 2.1–2). The history of the Church provides innumerable such instances, and thus we learn to ask those with more experience to judge whether our case is not merely imagination but grace proceeding from on High. We look for reliable witnesses who are to be found only in the Church whose age-old experience is immeasurably richer and more profound than our individual one. Such in the distant past were the apostles who bequeathed to us in gospel and epistle the knowledge which they had received direct from God. They were followed by a succession of fathers (doctors and ascetics) who handed down the centuries, above all, the spirit of life itself, often endorsing their testimony in writing. We believe that at any given historical moment it is possible to find living witnesses; to the end of time mankind will never be bereft of genuine gnosis concerning God. Only after authoritative confirmation may we trust our personal experience, and even then not to excess. Our spirit ought not to slacken in its impulse towards God. And at every step it is essential to remember that self-confident isolation is fraught with the possibility of transgressing against Truth. So we shall not cease to pray diligently to the Holy Spirit that He preserve our foot from the paths of untruth.

From the time of the apostles the faithful have lived in their prayer the single reality of One God in the Father, Son and Holy Spirit. Human language has never found satisfactory logical terminology for expressing spiritual experience and cognition of God as proclaimed by God Himself. All the words which new knowledge and new life have passed on from generation to

27

generation have to some extent or another clouded genuine contemplation of God. Consider, for example, two of the formulae for defining Unity. The one that we more generally meet with stresses unity of Substance. God is understood as One absolute Objectivity in Three absolute Subjects. To transfer the emphasis from Substance to Person—which is more consistent with the revelation I AM—the second theory interprets I AM as a Single absolute Subject combining in Himself I, Thou, We. (This is the assumption that Professor Bulgakov develops in his writings.) The first formula which purposes to demonstrate the plenitude of Divinity in each Hypostasis tends, as it were, to divide the Three. The second, in which the Personal principle is fundamental, leads to the fusion of the Persons.

The Church surmounted the inadequacy of our language by employing negative modes—teaching us to live the Persons of the Trinity 'neither confounding the Persons: nor dividing the Substance'. And where it is a question of the Incarnation of the Logos the definition becomes more complicated by the additions: 'not by conversion' ('of the Godhead into flesh'); 'without separation' ('One altogether . . . by unity of Person') [cf. Athanasian Creed]. Thus our rationally functioning mind is gripped in a vice, unable to incline to one side or the other, like a figure crucified on a cross.

Contemplation is a matter, not of verbal statements but of living experience. In pure prayer the Father, Son and Spirit are seen in their consubstantial unity.

The Gospel says, 'God so loved the world that he gave his only begotten Son, that whosoever believeth in him should not perish, but have everlasting life' (John 3.16). The Holy Spirit introduces us into the realm of Divine love, and we not only live this love but begin to understand that if God, the First and the Last, were mono-Hypostatic (that is, one Person), then He would not be love. Moses, who interpreted the revelation I AM as meaning a single hypostasis, gave his people the Law. But 'grace and truth came by Jesus Christ' (John 1.17). The Trinity is the God of love: 'The love of the Father which crucifies; the love of the Son which is crucified; the love of the Holy Spirit which is victorious' (Metropolitan Philaret of Moscow). Jesus, knowing 'that his hour was come that he should depart out of this world unto the Father, having loved his own which were in the world, he loved them *unto the end*' (John 13.1). This is our God. And there is none other save Him. The man who by the gift of the Holy Spirit has experienced the breath of His love knows with his whole being that such love is peculiar to the Triune Godhead revealed to us as the perfect mode of Absolute Being. The mono-Hypostatic God of the Old Testament and (long after the New Testament) of the Koran does not know love.

To love is to live for and in the beloved whose life becomes our life. Love leads to singleness of being. Thus it is within the Trinity. 'The Father loveth the Son' (John 3.35). He lives in the Son and in the Holy Spirit. The Son 'abides in the love of the Father' (John 15.10) and in the Holy Spirit. And the Holy Spirit we know as love all-perfect. The Holy Spirit proceeds eternally from the Father and lives in Him and abides in the Son. This love makes the sum total of Divine Being a single eternal Act. After the pattern of this unity mankind must also become one man. ('I and my Father are one' (John 10.30). 'That they all may be one; as Thou, Father, art in me, and I in thee, that they also may be one in us' (John 17.21).)*

Christ's commandment is the projection of heavenly love on the earthly plane. Realised in its true content, it makes the life of mankind similar to the life of the Triune God. The dawn of an understanding of this mystery comes with prayer for the whole world as for oneself. In this prayer one lives the consubstantiality of the human race. It is vital to proceed from abstract notions to existential—that is, ontological categories.

Within the life of the Trinity each Hypostasis is the Bearer of all the plenitude of Divine Being, and therefore dynamically equal to the Trinity as a whole. To achieve the fulness of god-man is to become dynamically equal to humanity in the aggregate. Herein

* This traditional theological concept is presented in more detail in my article *Unité de l'Eglise, image de la Sainte Trinité*. (*Messager de l'Exarchat*, 1950, no. 5: rue Pétel, Paris-XV.)

lies the true meaning of the second commandment, which is, indeed, 'like unto the first' (Matt. 22.39).

The integrality of the revelation given to us is inexhaustible. As created beings we are not able to know finally, completely, the uncreated First Being, in the way that God knows Himself. St Paul, however, looks forward in hope. 'For now we see through a glass, darkly . . . now I know in part; but then shall I know even as also I am known' (1 Cor. 13.12).

In the history of the Christian world we observe two theological tendencies: one, lasting for centuries, would accommodate the revelations concerning the Triune God to our manner of thinking; the other summons us to repentance, to a radical transformation of our whole being through life lived according to the Gospel. The former is laudable, even historically essential, but if separated from life it is doomed to failure. 'Jesus said . . . If a man love me, he will keep my words: and my Father will love him, and we will come unto him, and make our abode with him' (John 14.23). This is our Christian way to perfect gnosis. The abiding in us of the Father and the Son, and inseparable from Them the Holy Spirit, will give us true knowledge of God.

St Simeon the New Theologian (AD 949–1022) in his Hymn 17 cites the blind and unbelieving who do not accept the teaching of the Church that the Invisible, Incorruptible Creator came down to earth and united in Himself the two natures (the Divine and the created one of man), declaring that nobody of his own experience has known or lived this, or beheld it clearly. But in other hymns St Simeon repeats with the utmost conviction that such experience had been given to him again and again. When the imperishable Divine Light is imparted to man, man himself effectually becomes, as it were, light. The union of the two—of God and man—is accomplished by the Creator's will and in the consciousness of both. If this were to pass unrecognised, then, as St Simeon says, the union would be of the dead, not of the living. And how could eternal Life enter into man unperceived by him? How would it be possible, he continues, for Divine Light, like lightning in the night or a great sun, to shine in the heart and mind of man, and for man not to be aware of so sublime an event? Uniting with His likeness, God grants true knowledge of Himself as He is. Through the Holy Spirit the Son, too, is made known with the Father. And man beholds them in so far as he is able.

For us, Christians, Jesus Christ is the measure of all things, divine and human. 'In Him dwelleth the fulness of the Godhead' (Col. 2.9) and of mankind. He is our most perfect ideal. In Him we find the answer to all our problems, which without Him would be insoluble. He is in truth the mystical axis of the universe. If Christ were not the Son of God, then salvation through the adoption of man by God the Father would be totally incomprehensible. With Christ man steps forward into divine eternity.

3

The Risk in Creation

To produce something new is always a gamble, and God's creation of man in His image and after His likeness involved a certain degree of risk. It was not that He risked introducing an element of instability or shock into His Eternal Being but that to give man god-like freedom shut the door against predestination in any form. Man is at full liberty to determine himself negatively in relation to God—even to enter into conflict with Him. As infinite love, the Heavenly Father cannot abandon man whom He created for eternity, in order to impart to him His divine plenitude. He lives with us our human tragedy. We appreciate this risk, so breath-taking in its majesty, when we contemplate the life of Christ on earth.

After long study of Michelangelo's *Last Judgment* in the Sistine Chapel I discovered a partial analogy in the fresco with my conception of the Creation of the world. Look at Christ in the fresco, at the gesture He is making. Like some prize champion He hurls into the abyss all who have dared to oppose Him. The whole vast surface teems with people and angels trembling with fright. Suspended in some cosmic expanse, all are engrossed less with their own plight than with the wrath of Christ. He is in the centre and His anger is terrible. This, to be sure, is not how I see Christ. Michelangelo possessed great genius but not for liturgical subjects.

Let us reconstruct the fresco. Christ, naturally, must be in the centre, but a different Christ more in keeping with the revelation that we have of Him: Christ immensely powerful with the power of unassuming love. His is not a vindictive gesture. In creating us as free beings, He anticipated the likelihood, perhaps the inevitability, of the tragedy of the fall of man. Summoning us from the darkness of non-being, His fateful gesture flings us into the secret realms of cosmic life. 'In all places and fulfilling all things,' He stays for ever close to us. He loves us in spite of our senseless behaviour. He calls to us, is always ready to respond to our cries for help and guide our fragile steps through all the obstacles that lie in our path. He respects us as on a par with Him. His ultimate idea for us is to see us in eternity verily His equals, His friends and brothers, the sons of the Father. He strives for this, He longs for it. This is our Christ, and as Man He sat on the right hand of the Father.

In the beginning God creates our spirit as pure potential. What follows does not depend altogether on Him. Man is free to disagree, even to resist Him. A situation arises in which we ourselves determine our eternal future—always, of course, in relation to Him: without Him, we should not exist. And if we seek a hallowed eternity which essentially appertains to Him alone, then our every action, all our creative activity, must most certainly proceed not separately from Him but together with Him and in Him.

Born as pure potential, our spirit must go on to actualise our being as hypostasis. We need to grow, and this growth is linked with pain and suffering. However strange it may seem, suffering is imperative for the preservation of life created from nothing. If animals did not feel hunger, they would never make any effort to find food but would simply lie down and die. Similarly, acute discomfort compels primitive man to look for nourishment. Then, as he advances towards rational cognition, suffering discloses to his contemplative mind both his own imperfection and that of the world around him. This forces him to recognise the necessity for a new form of creative effort to perfect life in all its manifestations. Later, he will arrive at a certain perception of Supreme Being which will inspire his soul to seek for better knowledge of Him. And so on, until he realises that this Primordial Being, Whom apprehension first caused him to esteem, does not refuse congress with him; and in the light of this contact death is seen as an absurdity, the very possibility of which must be fought against relentlessly. And history has shown that many of those who waged this war with unflagging energy, even while they were still here on earth in spirit beheld the eternal kingdom of the Living God, and passed from death to unending life in the Light of Divine Being.

Let us consider again the dramatic gesture of 'our' Christ casting man whom He has created free, like a wonderful seed, into the world prepared for him. The movement is that of a sower throwing seed into the earth that has been ploughed and made ready.

The foundation-stone of our Christian theology is the revelation: 'In the beginning was the Word . . . and the Word was God . . . All things were made by him; and without him was not any thing made that was made. In him was life' (John 1.1,3,4). But contemporary science postulates that in the beginning was hydrogen, and from this atom, by an evolutionary process over milliards of years, everything else developed. The scientific principle—the objectification of the cosmos together with objective knowledge—is applicable only where the laws of nature prevail absolutely. It is not clear on what basis many scientists reject the possibility of other forms of being—of free, non-determined being. We know that Primordial Being lies outside the preserves of science, which can tell us nothing even of the meaning of our existence.

At all events, with both schools of thought, which differ so radically from each other, we notice two opposite tendencies in the human soul. Those on the one hand who abhor the, to them pointless, suffering associated with life on earth and, by extension, dislike existence in general, feel strangely drawn to the mysterious all-pervading quiescence of non-being. Others try to follow Christ; to dominate our earthly frailty and attain divine eternity, employing in their efforts to penetrate more profoundly into the secrets of unoriginate Being methods which may seem intolerably absurd. 'Not for that we would be unclothed, but clothed upon, that mortality might be swallowed up of life' (2 Cor. 5.4)—the opposite of the philosophy and ascetic theory of divestment of being.

34

We Christians accept the wondrous gift of life with thanksgiving. Called by Christ, we strive for the fullest possible knowledge of the Primary Source of all that exists. From our birth onwards we gradually grow and enter into possession of being. Christ is for us 'the way, the truth, and the life' (John 14.6). With Him our path lies through a great and intricate spiritual culture: we traverse cosmic chasms, more often with much suffering but not seldom in rapture as understanding increases. For a while the growing process is bound up with our physical body; but the time soon comes when, liberated from terrestrial chains, mind and spirit can continue their progress towards the Heavenly Father. We know that He loves us and because of this love reveals Himself to us without limit. It may still be only partly but we know that in Him is our immortality; in Him we shall arrive at everlasting Truth. He will grant us the indescribable joy of sharing in the very Act of the Divine creation of the world. We hunger for complete unity in Him. He is Light, Beauty, Wisdom, Love. He gives the noblest meaning to our life and the bliss of boundless gnosis.

The kind of personal being that we received at our birth—being as potentiality which we have in part already realised—could never develop from the hydrogen atom, in however many myriad years and whatever miraculous and unforeseen 'hazards' might happen. The ontological distance is too vast between the atom state of material being and that state of being which we already possess and which we are certain will be perfected and fulfilled.

It is natural that as Christians we should be exploring together in the perspective of the Gospel emphasis on our personal relationship with God. When the Holy Spirit by taking up His abode in us accords us to live the love commanded of us by Christ, we know in our bones that this is the only normal state for our immortal spirit; that in this state we comprehend the divine universality of Christ and His precepts. This is the Truth, the like of which leaves no room for doubt in heart or mind. It is the salvation taught us by the Church. (I speak now not of the ethical but of the ontological content of the Gospel.) This love is essentially a Divine Act, the power of which never diminishes but continues eternally in its plenitude.

When He took on our nature in its fallen state Christ, the Logos of the Father, restored it as it was and is for ever in the creative will of the Father. The incarnation of the only-begotten Son is the manifestation of the Divine in our form of being. Now is revealed the mystery of the way to salvation.

O GOD the FATHER Who art ever blessed;
Who hast called us to eternal glory in Jesus Christ,
Christ without sin, Who bore the sins of the world,
and laid His life on the cross that we might live for ever;
Who in the weakness of human flesh
made manifest the image of Thy perfection—
We beseech Thee, Father all-Holy,
fill us from on high with Thy strength,
that we may follow in His steps.
Make us like in goodness to Thy Son
in this proud, inconstant age,
that the way of Thy Truth suffer no blasphemy
because of our untruth,
nor be profaned by the sons of the adversary.

4

The Tragedy of Man

The tragedy of our times lies in our almost complete unawareness, or unmindfulness, that there are two kingdoms, the temporal and the eternal. We would build the Kingdom of Heaven on earth, rejecting all idea of resurrection or eternity. Resurrection is a myth. God is dead.

Let us go back to Biblical revelation, to the creation of Adam and Eve and the problem of original sin. 'God is light, and in him is no darkness at all' (1 John 1.5). The commandment given to the first-called in Paradise indicates this and at the same time conveys that, although Adam possessed absolute freedom of choice, to choose to eat of the tree of the knowledge of good and evil would entail a break with God as the sole source of life. By opting for knowledge of evil—in other words, by existentially associating with evil, by savouring evil—Adam inevitably broke with God, Who can in no way be joined with evil (*cf.* 2 Cor. 6.14–15). In breaking with God, Adam dies. 'In the day that thou eatest thereof,' thus parting company with me, rejecting my love, my word, my will, 'thou shalt surely die' (Gen. 2.17). Exactly how Adam 'tasted' the fruit of the tree of the knowledge of good and evil is not important. His sin was to doubt God, to seek to determine his own life independently of God, even apart from Him, after the pattern of Lucifer. Herein lies the essence of Adam's sin—it was a movement towards self-divinisation. Adam could naturally wish for deification—he had been created after the likeness of God—but he sinned in seeking this divinisation not through unity with God but through rupture. The serpent beguiled Eve, the helpmeet God had made for Adam, by suggesting that God was introducing a

37

prohibition which would restrict their freedom to seek divine plenitude of knowledge—that God was unwilling for them to 'be as gods knowing good and evil' (Gen. 3.5).

I first met with the notion of tragedy, not in life but in literature. The seeds of tragedy, it seemed to me in my youth, are sown when a man finds himself wholly captivated by some ideal. To attain this ideal he is ready to risk any sacrifice, any suffering, even life itself. But if he happens to achieve the object of his striving, it proves to be an impudent chimera: the reality does not correspond to what he had in mind. This sad discovery leads to profound despair, a wounded spirit, a monstrous death.

Different people have different ideals. There is the ambition for power, as with Boris Godounov. In pursuit of his aim he did not stop at bloodshed. Successful, he found that he had not got what he expected. 'I have reached the height of power but my soul knows no happiness.' Though the concerns of the spirit prompt a nobler quest, the genius in the realm of science or the arts sooner or later realises his inability to consummate his initial vision. Again, the logical *dénouement* is death.

The fate of the world troubled me profoundly. Human life at whatever stage was unavoidably interlinked with suffering. Even love was full of contradictions and bitter crises. The seal of destruction lay everywhere.

I was still a young man when the tragedy of historical events far outdid anything that I had read in books. (I refer to the outbreak of the First World War, soon to be followed by the Revolution in Russia.) My youthful hopes and dreams collapsed. But at the same time a new vision of the world and its meaning opened before me. Side by side with devastation I contemplated rebirth. I saw that there was no tragedy in God. Tragedy is to be found solely in the fortunes of the man whose gaze has not gone beyond the confines of this earth. Christ Himself by no means typifies tragedy. Nor are His all-cosmic sufferings of a tragic nature. And the Christian who has received the gift of the love of Christ, for all his awareness that it is not yet complete, escapes the nightmare of all-consuming death. Christ's love, during the whole time that He abode with us here, was acute suffering. 'O faithless and perverse generation,' He cried. 'How long shall I suffer you?' (Matt. 17.17). He wept for Lazarus and his sisters (*cf.* John 11.35). He grieved over the hard-heartedness of the Jews who slew the prophets (*cf.* Matt. 23.37). In Gethsemane his soul was 'exceeding sorrowful, even unto death' and 'his sweat was as it were great drops of blood falling down to the ground' (Matt. 26.38; Luke 22.44). He lived the tragedy of all mankind; but in Himself there was no tragedy. This is obvious from the words He spoke to His disciples perhaps only a short while before His redemptive prayer for all mankind in the Garden: 'My peace I give unto you' (John 14.27). And a little further on: 'I am not alone, because the Father is with me. These things I have spoken unto you, that in me ye might have peace. In the world ye shall have tribulation: but be of good cheer; I have overcome the world' (John 16.32,33). This is how it is with the Christian: for all his deep compassion, his tears and prayers for the world, there is none of the despair that destroys. Aware of the breath of the Holy Spirit, he is assured of the inevitable victory of Light. The love of Christ, even in the most acute stress of suffering (which I would call the 'hell of loving'), because it is eternal is free of passion. Until we achieve supreme freedom from the passions on this earth suffering and pity may wear out the body but it will only be the body that dies. 'Fear not them which kill the body, but are not able to kill the soul' (Matt. 10.28).

We may say that even today mankind as a whole has not grown up to Christianity and continues to drag out an almost brutish existence. In refusing to accept Christ as Eternal Man and, more importantly, as True God and our Saviour—whatever the form the refusal takes, and whatever the pretext—we lose the light of life eternal. 'Father, I will that they also, whom thou hast given me, be with me where I am; that they may behold my glory, which thou hast given me: for thou lovest me before the foundation of the world' (John 17.24). There, in the Kingdom of the Father and of the Son and of the Holy Spirit, must our mind dwell. We must hunger and thirst to enter into this wondrous Kingdom. Then we shall overcome in ourselves the sin of refusing the Father's love as revealed to us through the Son (*cf.* John 8.24).

When we choose Christ we are carried beyond time and space, beyond the reach of what is termed 'tragedy'.

The moment the Holy Spirit grants us to know the hypostatic form of prayer we can begin to break the fetters that shackle us. Emerging from the prison cell of selfish individualism into the wide expanse of life in the image of Christ, we perceive the nature of the personalism of the Gospel. Let us pause for a moment to examine the difference between these two theological concepts: the individual and the *persona*. It is a recognised fact that the ego is the weapon in the struggle for existence of the individual who refuses Christ's call to open our hearts to total, universal love. The *persona*, by contrast, is inconceivable without all-embracing love either in the Divine Being or in the human being. Prolonged and far from easy ascetic effort can open our eyes to the love that Christ taught, and we can apprehend the whole world through ourselves, through our own sufferings and searchings. We become like a world-wide radio receiver and can identify ourselves with the tragic element, not only in the lives of individual people but of the world at large, and we pray for the world as for our own selves. In this kind of prayer the spirit beholds the depths of evil, the sombre result of having eaten of the 'tree of the knowledge of good and evil'. But it is not only evil that we see—we make contact, too, with Absolute Good, with God, Who translates our prayer into a vision of Uncreated Light. The soul may then forget the world for whom she was praying, and cease to be aware of the body. The prayer of divine love becomes our very being, our body.

The soul may return to this world. But the spirit of man, having experienced his resurrection and come near existentially to eternity, is even further persuaded that tragedy and death are the consequence of sin and that there is no other way to salvation than through Christ.

5

Contemplation

What is the essence of Christian contemplation? How does it arise and where does it lead? Who or what is contemplated, and in what manner?

As I was taught, true contemplation begins the moment we become aware of sin in us. The Old Testament understood sin as the breach of the moral and religious precepts of the Law of Moses. The New Testament transferred the concept of sin to the inward man. To apprehend sin in oneself is a spiritual act, impossible without grace, without the drawing near to us of Divine Light. The initial effect of the approach of this mysterious Light is that we see where we stand 'spiritually' at the particular moment. The first manifestations of this Uncreated Light do not allow us to experience it as light. It shines in a secret way, illuminating the black darkness of our inner world to disclose a spectacle that is far from joyous for us in our normal state of fallen being. We feel a burning sensation. This is the beginning of real contemplation—which has nothing in common with intellectual or philosophical contemplation. We become acutely conscious of sin as a sundering from the ontological source of our being. Our spirit is eternal but now we see ourselves as prisoners of death. With death waiting at the end, another thousand years of life would seem but a deceptive flash.

Sin is not the infringement of the ethical standards of human society or of any legal injunction. Sin cuts us off from the God of Love made manifest to us as Light in Whom there is no darkness at all (cf. 1 John 1.5). To behold one's pitiful reality is a heavenly gift, one of the greatest. It means that we have already to a certain extent penetrated into the divine sphere, and have begun to contemplate—existentially, not philosophically—man as he is in God's idea of him before the creation of the world.

The horror of seeing oneself as one is acts as a consuming fire. The more thoroughly the fire performs its purifying work, the more agonising our spiritual pain. Yet, inexplicably, the unseen Light gives us a sense of divine presence within us: a strange secret presence that draws us to itself, to a state of contemplation which we know is genuine because our heart begins to throb day and night with prayer. It cannot be too often repeated that divine action has a twofold movement: one, which seems to us the first, plunges us into darkness and suffering. The other lifts us into the lofty spheres of the divine world. The range of our inner being expands and grows. But when the downward movement prevails, the cry is forced from us: 'It is a fearful thing to fall into the hands of the living God' (Heb. 10.31).

To begin with, we do not understand what is happening. Everything is new. We only later, and gradually, come to comprehend God's gift to us. Christ said to Peter: 'What I do thou knowest not now; but shalt know hereafter' (John 13.7). Impressed by the world revealed to her, which the heart did not yet know, the soul is both attracted and afraid. How can we describe the dread of losing God Who has so unexpectedly entered and enriched our life? Dismay at the thought of returning to the dark pit in which we existed until God's coming to us stimulates a desire to cleanse ourselves from all that could hinder the Spirit of God from taking up His abode in us for all eternity. This dismay is so immense that it brings total repentance.

Repentance does not come readily to carnal man; and none of us fathoms the problem of sin which is only disclosed to us through Christ and the Holy Spirit. The coming of the Holy Spirit is an event of supreme importance. Fallen man meets with God all-Holy. The notion of sin is possible only where God is regarded as Absolute Hypostasis. And, likewise, repentance for sin is possible and appropriate only where there is a personal relationship. Encounter with a Personal God—that is what the event signifies. The sinful man experiences at one and the same time fear and exultation. It is new birth from on High. An exquisite flower unfolds within us: the hypostasis—*persona*. Like the Kingdom of God the *persona* 'cometh not with observation' (Luke 17.20). The process whereby the human spirit enters into the domain of divine eternity differs with each one of us.

The soul comes to know herself first and foremost face to Face with God. And the fact that such prayer is the gift of God praying in us shows that the *persona* is born from on High and so is not subject to the laws of Nature. The *persona* transcends earthly bounds and moves in other spheres. It cannot be accounted for. It is singular and unique.

Absolute Being is Hypostatic; and man, the image of the Absolute, is hypostatic. God is Spirit, and man-hypostasis is spirit; yet spirit which is not unconnected, abstract, but given concrete expression by the corporal body. Just as the Divine Logos took on Himself human flesh and thereby showed that God is not a fantasy of man's imagination, born of ignorant fear of unknown phenomena, but actual reality. So, too, the human hypostasis is actually real. The Divine Spirit embraces all that exists. Man as hypostasis is a principle uniting the plurality of cosmic being; capable of containing the fulness of divine and human life.

The *persona* does not determine himself by opposition. His is an attitude of love. Love is the most profound content of his being, the noblest expression of his essence. In this love lies likeness to God, Who is Love. *Per se* the *persona* is excellence surpassing all other cosmic values. Rejoicing in the freedom that he has discovered, man contemplates the divine world.

Scientific and philosophical knowledge may be formulated but the *persona* is beyond definition and therefore incognisable from without, unless he himself reveals himself. Since God is a Secret God, so man has secret depths. He is neither the author of existence nor the end. God, not man, is the Alpha and Omega. Man's godlike quality lies in the mode of his being. Likeness in being is the likeness of which the Scriptures tell.

O Holy Trinity, Father, Son and Spirit;
Most High God, King and Creator of all eternity,

Who hast honoured us with Thy Divine image,
and didst describe in the visible form of our nature
the likeness of Thine invisible Being:
Enable us to find mercy and grace in Thy sight
that we may glorify Thee in the undying day of Thy
    kingdom,
with all Thy Saints throughout the ages.

When our spirit contemplates in itself the 'image and likeness' of God, it is confronted with the infinite grandeur of man, and not a few of us—the majority, perhaps—are filled with dread at our audacity.

In the Divine Being the Hypostasis constitutes the innermost esoteric principle of Being. Similarly, in the human being the hypostasis is the most intrinsic fundamental. *Persona* is 'the hidden man of the heart, in that which is not corruptible . . . which is in the sight of God of great price' (1 Peter 3.4)—the most precious kernel of man's whole being, manifested in his capacity for self-knowledge and self-determination; in his possession of creative energy; in his talent for cognition not only of the created world but also of the Divine world. Consumed with love, man feels himself joined with his beloved God. Through this union he knows God, and thus love and cognition merge into a single act.

God reveals Himself, mainly through the heart, as Love and Light. In this light man contemplates the Gospel precepts as the reflection on earth of celestial Eternity, and the Glory of Christ as of the only-begotten of the Father—the glory the disciples saw on Mount Tabor. The personal revelation makes the general revelation of the New Testament spiritually familiar.

This personal revelation may be granted suddenly. But though suddenly received man can only assimilate it by degrees, after long ascetic struggle. From the first instant the vital content of the revelation is clear and the soul feels no impulse to explain in rational concepts the grace experienced. But as a matter of course she aspires to ever deeper knowledge.

The divine nature of this personal vision is startlingly authentic, though words may fail to convey it. Yet the knowledge it offers has an objective *sui generis* character which we repeatedly observe down the centuries in the lives of many individuals largely identical in their experience and self-determining. 'Where two or three are gathered together' (Matt. 18.20)—there we have objectivity. 'There is none other name under heaven given among men, whereby we must be saved' (Acts 4.12), Peter declared categorically to the Sanhedrin. John spoke of 'that which was from the beginning, which we have heard, which we have seen with our eyes, which we have looked upon, and our hands have handled, of the Word of life' (1 John 1.1). And Paul who said that at present we know only 'in part' (1 Cor. 13.12), nevertheless decrees that 'if any man preach any other gospel unto you than that which we have preached unto you, let him be accursed' even though he be 'an angel from heaven' (Gal. 1.8,9).

As love, the hypostasis requires other hypostases. We see this from the revelation of the Holy Trinity. It is the same in the case of man. Having created Adam, 'the Lord God said, It is not good that the man should be alone' (Gen. 2.18). But can created being meet with the Creator? When the human *persona* stands before Him Who named Himself 'I AM THAT I AM' (Exos. 3.14), his spirit, his whole being not only glories but agonises over his own littleness, his ignorance, his wrong-doing. Suffering is his lot from the moment of his spiritual birth. Conscious that the process of transforming our whole earthly being is still far from complete, the spirit wearies.

Christian faith is the result of the presence within us of the Holy Spirit, and the soul knows Him. The Holy Spirit convinces the soul that she will not die; that death will not possess her. But the body, as the material instrument of the soul, is subject to decay.

Only sin can stifle the Divine breath within us. God Who is Holy does not blend with the darkness of sin. When we seek to justify a sinful action we *ipso facto* sever our alliance with God. God does not constrain us but neither can He be coerced. He retires, leaving us bereft of His luminous presence. Of course, man cannot altogether avoid sinning; but he can avoid the consequences of sin—separation from God—through repentance. With repentance and the consequent increase of grace within us, the reality of the

Divine World preponderates over the visible cosmos. We contemplate the FIRST REALITY.

O Father, Son, and Spirit;
Triune Godhead, One Being in three Persons;
Light unapproachable, Mystery most secret:
Lift our minds to contemplation of Thine unfathomable
    judgments
and fill our hearts with the light of Thy Divine love,
that we may serve Thee in spirit and truth
even unto our last breath.
We pray Thee, hear and have mercy.

6

Prayer of the Spirit

O Holy Spirit, All-powerful God;
Gracious Comforter and Almighty Defender;
Giver of Wisdom, and Light of Revelation;
Who by Thy descent didst bring
the uttermost parts of the world
to the only true knowledge of God:
Do Thou come down even upon us,
who grieve Thee always,
to enlighten and sanctify us,
to heal and comfort us
with Thine abiding comfort.

Misfortune in the shape of reduced circumstances, illness or the death of a loved one often drives people to prayer. But if the situation alters for the better, not only does their impulse to pray abate—prayer itself may seem pointless. But there is a different kind of prayer, prayer of the spirit, fastened on eternity, and here no external well-being can heal the sufferings of the soul who sees herself falling short of the sought-for eternal. Then prayer becomes the normal state for the soul, and the grace of the Holy Spirit may visit her, suddenly, inscrutably, bringing a foretaste of eternity. For this visitation integrity and faithfulness are the essential prerequisites. I have before me a remarkable document, a letter from a former rabbi.

'Why did I, a former rabbi, become a Christian?' he writes. 'The question sounds strange in my ears. Did I, of myself, become a Christian, following a plan, a purpose, after due

47

consideration? No, the grace of God made me Christian. My conversion is a mystery to me before which I bow my head in awe. It was the Holy Spirit, He alone transfigured me. When I accepted Christ the Laws of Deuteronomy ceased to be a means of drawing near to God . . . I feel myself all the time filled through and through with Divine love. Of a sudden, unexpectedly, independently of any effort of mine, light shone upon me—the light that in the old days when I was a devout Jew was only a far-off glimmer. All at once I beheld in myself the Holy One, the Mystery of Mysteries and yet the clearest of all that is clear . . . As for religious ethics, they are much the same in Judaism as in Christianity: the commandments concerning morals are often expressed in identical terms. In practice, however, they differ vitally. The Christian ethic is given from on High, by the Holy Spirit, Who came to us only after Christ's resurrection. It is the same Spirit that pious Jews dream of to this day: they feel Him, see Him, but only *from afar*. But the true Christian lives in the Holy Spirit through faith in Jesus Christ. The Holy Spirit captivates even our body with the sweetest love, liberating it from thraldom to the passions until the body itself longs to dissolve in the Spirit. And so it was not I of myself who became Christian—it was God Who sent down the grace of the Holy Spirit and made me so . . . The Spirit reposes within the true Christian and encircles him round about. And all this happens through faith in Christ. This is the process: faith attracts the Holy Spirit, while the Holy Spirit strengthens faith, cares for you, sustains you, encourages your ardent desire for the Kingdom of God . . . To those who have not yet savoured true grace, my words will be unintelligible. The process of true conversion cannot be described or explained: it is something that the eye cannot see, that the ear cannot hear. Filled with Christian sentiments, I heard my soul speaking within me, telling me of my new birth in Christ; but she spoke in the language of silence which I cannot find words for. I do know, though, that my soul sang a new song, a sweet song of love which lifted the power of the past from me. And this song transfigured me and gave birth in me to a new will, to new

48

yearnings. Now I am as it were in love with Christ, and, you know, a man in love with Christ has no desire to philosophise. He only wants one thing—to love for all eternity. Do you want to understand? Would you like to experience the grace of Christ? Then seek this grace from Him Who can bestow it. If it seems that it is not for you, since you cannot believe, my advice is to set your heart on believing and you will be able to believe. Through faith you arrive at faith. Persist in wishing for faith and it will be granted to you. When I was a Jew I, too, had God and knew it. But it was a God Whose attitude changed according to man's conduct. But through Christ, through the Holy Messiah and Son of God, I was led into the sphere of unconditional, steadfast Divine love. This can only be understood if you already live in grace. Christianity is the richest of treasures equal to satisfying each and every soul.

'In Christ is Truth, to which the Holy Spirit bears witness. And all who believe heed His testimony.'

I have quoted this triumphant cry of a soul who found the Christ-God because, though many have had a similar experience, few find words to express the well-nigh inexpressible.

The Holy Spirit comes when we are receptive. He does not compel. He approaches so meekly that we may not even notice. If we would know the Holy Spirit we need to examine ourselves in the light of the Gospel teaching, to detect any other presence which may prevent the Holy Spirit from entering into our souls. We must not wait for God to force Himself on us without our consent. God respects and does not constrain man. It is amazing how God humbles Himself before us. He loves us with a tender love, not haughtily, not with condescension. And when we open our hearts to Him we are overwhelmed by the conviction that He is indeed our Father. The soul then worships in love.

St Gregory of Sinai goes so far as to say that prayer is God Himself acting in us. 'Do Thou Thyself pray in me,' was the constant appeal of Philaret, Metropolitan of Moscow in the last century. We also have the witness of St Paul: 'And because ye are

49

sons, God hath sent forth the Spirit of his Son into your hearts, crying, Abba, Father' (Gal. 4,6).

Fired by the vision of our high calling, we strain to accomplish our purpose—our yearning for Divine love to dwell in us for ever. Without this preliminary rapture of faith, without this fervent reaching towards the loving God Who continually inspires us, we cannot help falling beneath the massive pressure of the contemporary world which does not know prayer.

Life-giving faith consists in unquestioning belief in Christ as God. Only when Christ is accepted as perfect God and perfect Man does the plenitude of spiritual experience described by the apostles and fathers become possible. Christ is now the corner-stone on which we must construct our entire life, both temporal and eternal. The nature of the gifts which such faith entrains declares their supernal provenance.

The Lord said: 'But thou, when thou prayest, enter into thy closet and when thou hast shut the door, pray to thy Father which is in secret: and thy Father which seeth in secret shall reward thee openly' (Matt. 6.6). True prayer operates in our innermost depths which we learn to hide from outside eyes. If I now venture to touch on matters sacred for each of us, I am urged to do so by the tragic atmosphere of tension throughout the world, and, more especially, by my consciousness that we belong together in Christ. Let us, therefore, as true brethren, share what it has been given us to know by a gift from on High. (I would ask you to pray as you read, as I pray God to inspire me with words pleasing to Him.)

Christ gave us the word that He had received from the Father (cf. John 17.14). He spoke of Himself as the stone which will break all who fall on it and will grind to powder those on whom it falls (cf. Matt. 21.44). What then? Is it we who have fallen on this great and wondrous stone, or has the stone fallen on us? We do not know. But however that may be, we are precipitated into a world of realities whose existence we did not suspect before. In the old days when life for the majority flowed in the broad chan-nels of established tradition, the word of Christ was so presented as not to disturb. But now, with the whole earth full fraught with man's despair, with the protest of consciences outraged, with violence threatening to wipe out all life, we must needs make our voices heard. In our present peril decorous words which commit us to nothing are not enough. All of us today are in vital need of a firm faith in Christ's eternal victory, that we, too, may become spiritually invincible. A very great deal depends on ourselves—to remember, for instance, that at the baptismal font we received new birth from on High, in the Name of the Father and of the Son and of the Holy Spirit. Those who are baptised 'with the Holy Ghost and with fire' (Luke 3.16) perceive in their prayer that every given moment of our life is enveloped in Divine eternity. At all times and in all places we are held in the invisible Hand of our Heavenly Father.

It is usual for the Christian to be aware concurrently of the presence of the never-fading celestial glory and of the brooding cloud of death hanging over the world. Though the feeling of death torments the soul, it cannot extinguish the fire of faith. The prayer throbbing within us sets us on the frontier between two worlds, the transient and the one to come (cf. Heb. 13.14). This painful rending forces us into still more fervent entreaty. We recognise our sickness—the mortal power of sin working in us—and plead for a physician. Then He Who said that He was 'not come to call the righteous, but sinners to repentance', adding that 'they that be whole need not a physician, but they that are sick' (Matt. 9.12,13), does indeed answer our appeal. He heals our souls from every ill, giving new energy, enlightening with an undying light. The age-old experience of life in the Church has proved irrefutably that for prayer—that is, for God—no sickness of spirit is incurable. We may be born into the most unfavourable circumstances. We may grow up in ignorant, rough, even criminal surroundings, and be attracted by the general example. We may suffer every kind of deprivation, loss, injury. We may be deformed from birth, and know what it is to be despised, wounded, rejected. All that is unfortunate in the contemporary world may make its mark on us, possess us, even; but from the moment we turn to God, resolved to follow His commandments, a process of basic healing begins. And not only are we healed of our wounds or passions—

even our outward appearance may alter. This happened often on the Holy Mountain. Men would arrive broken and reduced to a pitiful state by many years of depraved living, yet after a brief period of profound repentance their faces were good to look upon, their voices changed, they moved differently—and the spirit shone luminous within them. If any of my readers is suffering from some psychological wound occasioned by failure in life, he can attain to a regal freedom of spirit and radically change his whole life if he turns to God every day with a personal prayer such as this, for example:

Prayer at Daybreak

O Lord Eternal and Creator of all things,
Who of Thine inscrutable goodness didst call me to this life;
Who didst bestow on me the grace of Baptism
and the Seal of the Holy Spirit;
Who hast imbued me with the desire to seek Thee,
the one true God: hear my prayer.

I have no life, no light, no joy or wisdom;
no strength except in Thee, O God.
Because of my unrighteousness I dare not raise my eyes to
    Thee.
But Thou didst say to Thy disciples,
'Whatsoever ye shall ask in prayer believing, ye shall receive'
and 'Whatsoever ye shall ask in my name, that will I do'.
Wherefore I dare to invoke Thee.
Purify me from all taint of flesh and spirit.
Teach me to pray aright.

Bless this day which Thou dost give unto me,
Thine unworthy servant. By the power of Thy blessing
enable me at all times to speak and act to Thy glory
with a pure spirit, with humility, patience, love,
gentleness, peace, courage and wisdom:
aware always of Thy presence.

Of Thine immense goodness, O Lord God, shew me the
    path of Thy will,
and grant me to walk in Thy sight without sin.

O Lord, unto Whom all hearts be open,
Thou knowest what things I have need of.
Thou art acquainted with my blindness and my ignorance,
Thou knowest my infirmity and my soul's corruption;
but neither are my pain and anguish hid from Thee.
Wherefore I beseech Thee, hear my prayer
and by Thy Holy Spirit teach me the way wherein I should
    walk;
and when my perverted will would lead me down other paths
spare me not, O Lord, but force me back to Thee.
By the power of Thy love, grant me to hold fast to that which is
    good.
Preserve me from every word or deed that corrupts the soul;
from every impulse unpleasing in Thy sight
and hurtful to my brother-man.
Teach me what I should say and *how* I should speak.
If it be Thy will that I make no answer,
inspire me to keep silent in a spirit of peace
that causeth neither sorrow nor hurt to my fellow.
Establish me in the path of Thy commandments
and to my last breath let me not stray from the light of Thine
    ordinances,
that Thy commandments may become the sole law of my being
on this earth and in all eternity.

Yea, Lord, I pray Thee, have pity on me.
Spare me in mine affliction and my misery
and hide not the way of salvation from me.

In my foolishness, O God, I plead with Thee for many and
    great things.
Yet am I ever mindful of my wickedness, my baseness, my
    vileness.
Have mercy upon me.
Cast me not away from Thy presence because of my presump-
    tion.
Do Thou rather increase in me this presumption,

and grant unto me, the worst of men,
to love Thee as Thou hast commanded,
with all my heart, and with all my soul,
and with all my mind, and with all my strength:
with my whole being.

Yea, O Lord, by Thy Holy Spirit,
teach me good judgment and knowledge.
Grant me to know Thy truth before I go down into the grave.
Maintain my life in this world until I may offer unto Thee
    worthy repentance.
Take me not away in the midst of my days,
nor while my mind is still blind.
When Thou shalt be pleased to bring my life to an end,
forewarn me that I may prepare my soul to come before Thee.
Be with me, O Lord, at that dread hour
and grant me the joy of salvation.
Cleanse Thou me from secret faults,
from all iniquity that is hid in me;
and give me a right answer before Thy judgment-seat.

Yea, Lord, of Thy great mercy
and immeasurable love for mankind,

Hear my prayer

To pray like that every morning is not easy. But if we pray
from our heart, with all our attention, the day will be stamped by
our prayer and everything that happens will take on a different
character. The blessing that we have sought from the High God
will beget a gentle peace in our soul which will have a miraculous
effect on the way we see and interpret the world. The man of
prayer beholds the surrounding scene in another light. Concern
is quickened and the intrinsic quality of life enhanced. In time
prayer will penetrate our nature until gradually a new man is born
of God. Love for God, Who verily sends His blessing upon us,
liberates the soul from extraneous pressure. The one imperative is

to preserve this loving tie with God. We shall not care what people think of us, or how they treat us. We shall cease to be afraid of falling out of favour. We shall love our fellow men without thought of whether they love us. Christ gave us the commandment to love others but did not make it a condition of salvation that they should love us. Indeed, we may positively be disliked for independence of spirit. It is essential in these days to be able to protect ourselves from the influence of those with whom we come in contact. Otherwise we risk losing both faith and prayer. Let the whole world dismiss us as unworthy of attention, trust or respect —it will not matter provided that the Lord accepts us. And vice versa: it will profit us nothing if the whole world thinks well of us and sings our praises, if the Lord declines to abide with us. This is only a fragment of the freedom Christ meant when He said, 'Ye shall know the truth, and the truth shall make you free' (John 8.32). Our sole care will be to continue in the word of Christ, to become His disciples and cease to be servants of sin. For 'whosoever committeth sin is the servant of sin. And the servant abideth not in the house for ever: but the Son abideth ever. If the Son therefore shall make you free, ye shall be free indeed' (John 8.34–36). The end result of prayer is to make us sons of God, and as sons we shall abide for ever in the house of our Father. 'Our Father which art in heaven . . .'

Real prayer, of course, does not come readily. It is no simple matter to preserve inspiration while surrounded by the icy waters of the world that does not pray. Christ cast the Divine Fire on earth, and we pray Him so to fire our hearts that we may not be overcome even by cosmic cold, that no black cloud blot out the bright flame.

Of all approaches to God prayer is the best and in the last analysis the only means. In the act of prayer the human mind finds its noblest expression. The mental state of the scientist engaged in research, of the artist creating a work of art, of the thinker wrapped up in philosophy—even of professional theologians propounding their doctrines—cannot be compared to that of the man of prayer brought face to Face with the living God. Each and every kind of mental activity presents less of a strain than prayer. We may be capable of working for ten or twelve hours on end but a few moments of prayer and we are exhausted.

Prayer can accomplish all things. It is possible for any of us lacking in natural talent to obtain through prayer supranatural gifts. Where we encounter a deficiency of rational knowledge we should do well to remember that prayer, independently of man's intellectual capacity, can bring a higher form of cognition. There is the province of reflex consciousness, of demonstrative argument; and there is the province where prayer is the passageway to direct contemplation of divine truth.

There is a pronounced tendency among scientists of the present century to claim integral knowledge of the natural world. 'The sum total of all that is already known emphasises the unlimited capacity of the human mind, and proves that every natural phenomenon is cognizable,' declared a Russian scientist in 1958. We, Christians, similarly aspire to integral knowledge of being, in the deepest and widest sense. The world of matter does not yet encompass plenitude of being. Without belittling the importance of experimental science, of vital necessity, perhaps, in the struggle for existence, we still cannot overlook its limitations. I once heard the following story of a professor of astronomy who was enthusiastically discoursing in a planetarium on the nebulae and like marvels. Noticing an unpretentious priest who had joined his group of students, the professor asked him:

'What do your Scriptures say about cosmic space and its myriad stars?'

Instead of giving a direct answer the priest in turn posed a question.

'Tell me, Professor,' he said, 'do you think that science will invent still more powerful telescopes to see even farther into the firmament?'

'Of course progress is possible and science will always be perfecting apparatus for exploring outer space,' replied the astronomer.

'There is hope, then, that one day you will have telescopes that can show all there is in the cosmos, down to the last detail?'

'That would be impossible—the cosmos is infinite,' replied the scientist.

'So there is a limit to science?'

'Yes, in that sense, there is.'

'Well, Professor,' said the priest, 'where your science comes to a full stop, ours begins, and that is what our Scriptures tell of.'

7

The Bliss of Knowing the Way

'O Israel, happy are we: for things that are pleasing to God are made known unto us. Be of good cheer, my people' (*Apocrypha*: Baruch 4.4,5). And if we consider how much more we Christians are endowed by the Lord than were the prophets and righteous men of the Old Testament, we, too, must lift up our voices and cry in grateful triumph: 'Blessed are we, hallowed Christians, for the Lord hath desired so to be united with us that His life is become ours.'

The Lord Himself bore witness to this when He told the disciples: 'Blessed are your eyes, for they see: and your ears, for they hear. For verily I say unto you, That many prophets and righteous men have desired to see those things which ye see, and have not seen them, and to hear those things which ye hear, and have not heard them' (Matt. 13.16,17). And St Peter declared that to the prophets 'it was revealed that not unto themselves, but unto us they did minister the things, which are now reported unto you by them that have preached the gospel unto you with the Holy Ghost sent down from heaven', adding, so great were the good tidings, 'which things the angels desire to look into' (1 Pet. 1.12).

St Paul, also, in his epistle to the Ephesians, wrote that 'knowledge in the mystery of Christ which in other ages was not made known unto the sons of men . . . was now revealed unto his holy apostles and prophets by the Spirit' (*cf.* Eph. 3), and went on to tell them that to him had been given grace to 'preach among the Gentiles the unsearchable riches of Christ; and to make all men see what is the fellowship of the mystery, which from the beginning of the world hath been hid in God'. So tremendous, so profound is the mystery that even to the 'principalities and powers in heavenly places the manifold wisdom of God must be made known by the church according to the eternal purpose which the Father purposed in Christ Jesus our Lord: In whom we have boldness and access with confidence by the faith of him.'

In our day non-Christian mysticism attracts many who despair at the banality and emptiness of the contemporary scene. They are ignorant of the true essence of Christianity. Christianity entails suffering; but through suffering we penetrate the mysteries of Being. Suffering makes it possible to comprehend one's own humanity and freedom. In times of distress the Christian remembers that 'the whole creation groaneth and travaileth in pain' (Rom. 8.22) and his spirit is conscious of the same life flowing through all of us. To extend the range of our consciousness makes us kin with millions of fellow-beings scattered over the face of the earth. An enhanced recognition of human suffering begets intense prayer which transfers all things into the realm of the spirit.

I once read a newspaper account of an engineer testing the jet engine of a 'plane who carelessly stepped into the air stream which caught and lifted him high off the ground. Seeing what had happened, his assistant quickly switched off the engine. The mechanic fell to the ground, dead. Something similar happens to the man of prayer: after being caught up into another sphere he returns to earth 'dead' to much that is of this world. A new life full of light has manifested itself in him, and now the infantile pastimes which occupy the vast majority cease to hold any interest or attraction for him. If we assess the quality of life not by the sum of agreeable psycho-physical sensations but by the extent of our awareness of the realities of the universe and, above all, of the First and Last Truth, we shall understand what lay behind Christ's words, 'My peace I give unto you'—said to the disciples a few hours before His death on the cross. The essence of Christ's peace lies in His perfect knowledge of the Father. So it is with us: if we know the Eternal Truth all the torments of this life will be confined, as it were, to the periphery of our being, while the light of life proceeding from the Father will reign within us.

No success or temporary well-being can bring genuine peace if we continue ignorant of Truth. There are not many people with enough spiritual courage to step aside from the trite path followed by the herd. Courage is born of steadfast belief in Christ-God. 'This is the victory that overcometh the world, even our faith' (1 John 5.4).

Those with no experience of prayer find it hard to believe how prayer broadens the horizons of the spirit. Sometimes prayer consumes the heart like fire; and when the heart succumbs to the burning flame, unexpectedly there falls the dew of divine consolation. When we become so conscious of our frailty that our spirit despairs, somehow, in an unknown fashion, a wondrous light appears, proclaiming life incorruptible. When the darkness within us is so appalling that we are paralysed with dread, the same light will turn black night into bright day. When we properly condemn ourselves to eternal infamy and in agony descend into the pit, of a sudden some strength from Above will lift our spirit to the heights. When we are overwhelmed by the feeling of our own utter nothingness, the uncreated light transfigures and brings us like sons into the Father's house.

How are these contrasting states to be explained? Why does our self-condemnation justify us before God? Is it not because there is truth in this self-condemnation and so the Spirit of Truth finds a place for Himself in us?

Even remote contact with the Divine releases the soul from all passions, including envy, that vile offspring of pride. The man who continues with a humble opinion of himself will be given greater knowledge of the mysteries of the world to come. He will be delivered from the power of death. United through prayer with Christ, he realises that in eternity the whole content of being will belong to him, too, through the perpetual dwelling in him of the Holy Spirit—of the Trinity, it would be truer to say. Father, Son and Holy Spirit will make Their abode with him. By virtue of this, every good word or deed, from whatever source, will become part of his eternal divinised life. Thus, in the words of St Paul 'as having nothing yet we possess all things' (2 Cor. 6.10). If anyone performs deeds to the glory of God which bring him both temporal and eternal renown, the man of prayer feels not envy but joy at our common salvation. My brother's glory will be my glory, also. What blessedness to behold fellow humans radiant with the Holy Spirit! Yet even this is but a pale reflection of our joy in the Kingdom to come where, in a superabundance of love which never diminishes, the spirit of man will embrace the fulness of god-man being.

Let us not forget, however, that the way to this superabundant love lies through the depths of hell. We must not be afraid of this descent since without it plenitude of knowledge is unobtainable.

Sometimes the trials and difficulties which befall put us in the position of a traveller who suddenly finds himself on the edge of an abyss from which it is impossible to turn back. The abyss is the darkness of ignorance, and terror at being captive to death. Only the energy of a saintly despair will get us across. Upheld by some mysterious strength, we cast ourselves into the unknown, calling upon the Name of the Lord. And what happens? Instead of smashing our heads against unseen rocks, we feel an invisible hand gently carrying us over, and we come to no harm. Throwing ourselves into the unknown means trusting to God, having let go of all hope in the great ones of the earth, and setting off in search of a new life in which first place is given to Christ.

Traversing the abyss of the unknown can also be likened to swinging along a cable stretched from one side to the other. The hands of Christ crucified link the far ends of the abyss. The soul that has been given the dread privilege of travelling along this cable can find no words to describe it, just as those who have passed beyond the grave cannot tell us of their experience on the new plane.

The spiritual vision just outlined dissolves into contemplation of the crucified Christ. His arms are outstretched to gather all peoples into one, to link the far corners of the world; His body, hanging on the cross, forms a stupendous bridge between earth and heaven. Uniting in Himself both God and Man, He calls upon us to follow in His steps. It is not a simple matter to portray what meets the spiritual eye at such times. Just as a heavy body precipitated beyond the range of terrestrial gravity becomes subject to the mechanics of space and moves at a speed impossible on the surface of the earth, so it is with our spirit when prayer in its upsurge towards God overcomes the passions which pin us down, to move in the luminous sphere of the Divine and contemplate the sublime and hitherto unknown. In the depths of our consciousness we apprehend the unoriginate Truth, and the Spirit testifies to our immortality. Thus the first dread vision of darkness and mortality changes to a vision of light and life indestructible.

The touch of Divine love in the heart is our first contact with the heavenly side of the abyss. Delivered from the power of death, our spirit no longer trembles in the face of death. Nevertheless, the love that has entered the soul is not free from fear of another kind—fear of somehow hurting a fellow-being and, perhaps even more, of grieving the Holy Spirit by an impulse of the heart, a thought or a word. Only through a more abundant measure of grace which manifests itself in love for enemies does the spirit become kin, as it were to God. Yet even with such love as this we can still run into difficulties with people, since the very presence of divine action within us in a strange fashion provokes hostility in those who do not love God. There is no deeper, more tragic conflict than the conflict between this world of ours and Christ.

Those who are not reborn from on High will never understand those who are. There appears to be nothing outstanding about Christians, who may often seem morbid or hypocritical. The regenerated soul is more sensitive to all spiritual phenomena— more deeply wounded by all that is contrary to divine love: by calumny, violence, murder and so on. Together with this, a patient attitude to every ordeal makes the regenerated soul more able to apprehend the 'wisdom that is from above' (Jas. 3.17). In some hidden place within her she finds 'a well of water springing up into everlasting life' (John 4.14). Prayer is like a strong hand clinging fast to God's raiment, at all times and in all places: in the turmoil of the crowd, in the pleasant hours of leisure, in periods of loneliness.

At first the struggle for prayer seems to be beyond our strength but if she persists the soul will eventually be able to contain within herself at the same time sorrow and joy; despair and hope. There is no more alternating between elation and depression, since all states are gathered into a single whole. Through knowledge of God the soul has acquired profound peace.

Strange are the ways of the Lord. Man by himself cannot discover them. God, by His appearance, revealed to us the peculiar path to eternal salvation. He gave us an example in all things. He taught us how the Holy Spirit acts in us. He filled us with imperishable light away from which there is no true knowledge anywhere, no salvation for anyone. From Him we learned of the unlimited possibilities for those who were created in His image.

O God and Father, without beginning;
Thou Who art blessed throughout all ages;
Who hast revealed unto us the mystery
of the way of Thy salvation:
Renew our nature, by Thy Word abiding in us,
and make us the temple of Thy Holy Spirit,
that being ever guarded by Thy might
we may give glory to Thee in a worthy manner,
now and for ever.

8

The Struggle in Prayer

O Holy Spirit, Eternal King
and Giver of life incorruptible:
Look down in Thine infinite mercy
on the infirmities of our nature.
Illumine and hallow us.
Let the light of Thy knowledge
shine forth in our darkened hearts.
And in the earthen vessels of our nature
manifest Thine invincible strength.

Prayer is infinite creation, the supreme art. Over and over again we experience an eager upsurge towards God, followed only by a falling away from His light. Time and again we are conscious of the mind's inability to rise to Him. There are moments when we feel ourselves on the verge of insanity. 'Thou didst give me Thy precept to love but there is no strength in me for love. Come and perform in me all that Thou hast commanded, for Thy commandment overtaxes my powers. My mind is too frail to comprehend Thee. My spirit cannot see into the mysteries of Thy will. My days pass in endless conflict. I am tortured by the fear of losing Thee because of the evil thoughts in my heart.'

Sometimes prayer seems to flag and we cry, 'Make haste unto me, O God' (Ps. 70.5). But if we do not let go of the hem of His garment, help will come. It is vital to *dwell* in prayer in order to counteract the persistently destructive influence of the outside world.

Prayer cannot fail to revive in us the divine breath which God breathed into Adam's nostrils and by virtue of which Adam 'became a living soul' (Gen. 2.7). Then our regenerated spirit will marvel at the sublime mystery of being, and our hearts echo the Psalmist's praise of the wonderful works of the Lord. We shall apprehend the meaning of Christ's words, 'I am come that [men] might have life, and that they might have it more abundantly' (John 10.10).

But this life is full of paradox, like all the Gospel teaching. 'I am come to send fire on earth; and what will I, if it be already kindled?' (Luke 12.49). Unless we go through this fire that consumes the decaying passions of our nature, we shall not see the fire transformed into light, for it is not Light that comes first, then Fire: in our fallen state burning precedes enlightenment. Let us, therefore, bless God for this consuming fire. We do not know altogether but we do at least know 'in part' (1 Cor. 13.9) that there is no other way for us mortals to become 'children of the resurrection' (Luke 20.36), to reign together with Christ. However painful this re-creating may be; however it may distress and lacerate—the process, agonising as it is, will be a blessed one. Erudition requires long labour but prayer is incalculably harder to acquire.

When the Gospels and Epistles become real for us we see how naïve were our past notions of God and life in Him, so far does Reality surpass man's imagining. 'Eye hath not seen, nor ear heard, neither have entered into the heart of man, the things which God hath prepared for them that love him' (1 Cor. 2.9). Even a whisper of the Divine is glory beyond compare to all the content of life lived apart from God.

Strait is the way, and thorny and sorrowful. We shall heave many a sigh as we go along. The peculiar fear which is 'the beginning of wisdom' (Ps. 111.10) will clutch at our heart and twist our whole being outside in to concentrate attention on what is happening within. Impotent to follow Christ, we stop short in dread. 'Jesus went before [the disciples]; they were amazed; and as they followed, they were afraid' (Mark 10.32).

None of us can escape suffering if we would be born into a new life in God—if we would transform our natural body into a spiritual body. (As St Paul said, 'It is sown a natural body; it is raised a spiritual body' (1 Cor. 15.44).) Only the power of prayer overcomes the resistance of matter and releases our spirit from this cramped, inert world into the vast open spaces radiant with Light.

The mind is bewildered by the trials that befall in our struggle for prayer. It is not easy to identify their cause or their kind. Until we go 'into the sanctuary of God' (Ps. 73.17) we shall often hesitate, unsure whether our works are pleasing to the All-Holy. Since we are not exempt from sin we can only think that it is our wrong-doing which provokes the storms raging around us— though St Peter reminded the early Christians in their despair that 'the spirit of glory' (1 Pet. 4.14) rested upon them. One thing, however, is not open to doubt: the hour will come when all our trials and tribulations will disappear into the past. Then we shall see that the most painful periods of our life were the most fruitful and will accompany us beyond the confines of this world, to be the foundation of the Kingdom 'which cannot be moved' (Heb. 12.28).

The omnipotent God summoned us from the void. By nature we are of the void; yet even from God we expect consideration and regard. Suddenly the Almighty reveals Himself in boundless humility. The vision floods our entire being and instinctively we bow in adoration. Even this does not seem enough but however much we try to humble ourselves before Him we still fall short of His humility.

Prayer to this God of love and humility rises from the depths of our being. When our heart is filled with love for God we are wholly aware of our closeness to Him—although we know full well that we are but dust (cf. Gen. 3.19). Howbeit, in the visible form of our nature the immortal God described the likeness of His invisible Being, and thus we apprehend eternity. Through prayer we enter into Divine life; and God praying in us is un-created life permeating us.

In making us in His image, after His likeness, God placed us before Him, not as action of His, entirely subject to Him, but as *fact* (*datum*) even for Him—as free beings And by virtue of this, relations between man and God are based on the principle of freedom. When we take advantage of this freedom and commit sin, we thrust God aside. This liberty to turn away from God is the negative, tragic aspect of free will but it is a *sine qua non* if we are to take hold of the life which is truly divine, life which is not predetermined.

We have the diametrically opposite alternatives: either to refuse God—the very essence of sin—or to become sons of God. Because we are made in the likeness of God we naturally desire the divine perfection which is in our Father. And when we follow Him we are not submitting to the dictates of some extraneous power: we are merely obeying our own impulse to assimilate His perfection. 'Be ye therefore perfect, even as your Father which is in heaven is perfect' (Matt. 5.48).

Our Father which art in heaven,
Hallowed be thy Name
    Thou hast given me to perceive Thy holiness, and I would fain be holy in Thee.
Thy kingdom come
    May Thy glorious life enter into me and become mine.
Thy will be done
    in the earth of my created being, as it is in heaven, in Thee Thyself, from all eternity.
Give us this day our daily bread
    'the true bread which cometh down from heaven, and giveth life unto the world' (John 6.32–33).
And forgive us our trespasses, As we forgive them that trespass against us
    By Thy Holy Spirit grant me so to forgive others that nothing may prevent me from receiving Thy forgiveness.
Lead us not into temptation
    Thou knowest my perverseness; that I am ever ready to transgress. Send Thine angel to stand in the way for an adversary against me when I would sin (*cf.* Num. 22.22).
But deliver us from evil
    Deliver me from the power of the mortal enemy, the adversary of man and God.

At first we pray for ourselves; but when God by the Holy Spirit gives us understanding our prayer assumes cosmic proportions. Then, when we pray 'Our Father' we think of all mankind, and solicit fulness of grace for all as for ourselves. Hallowed be Thy Name among all peoples. Thy kingdom come for all peoples that Thy Divine life may become their life. Thy will be done: Thy will alone unites all in love of Thee. Deliver us from evil—from 'the murderer' (John 8.44) who, far and wide, sows enmity and death. (According to our Christian interpretation evil—like good—exists only where there is personal form of being. Without this personal form there would be no evil—only determined natural processes.)

The problem of evil in the world generally and in mankind particularly poses the question of God's participation in the historical life of the human race. Many lose their faith because it seems that, if God existed, evil could not be so rampant and there could not be such widespread senseless suffering. They forget that God cares for man's freedom, which is the root principle of his creation in the Divine image. For the Creator to interfere when man inclines to evil would be tantamount to depriving him of the possibility of self-determination, and would destroy him altogether. But God can and does save individuals and nations if they tread the road He designates.

Christ said, 'I came not to send peace, but a sword' (Matt. 10.34) and 'division' (Luke 12.51). Christ summoned us to war on the plane of the spirit, and our weapon is 'the sword of the Spirit, which is the word of God' (Eph. 6.17). Our battle is waged in extraordinarily unequal conditions. We are tied hand and foot. We dare not strike with fire or sword: our sole armament is love, even for enemies. This unique war in which we are engaged is indeed a holy war. We wrestle with the last and only enemy of mankind—death (1 Cor. 15.26). Our fight is the fight for universal resurrection.

The Lord justified and sanctified the line of His forefathers. Likewise, every one of us, if we follow Christ, can justify ourselves in our individual being, having restored the Divine image in us through total repentance, and by so doing can help to justify our own forefathers. We bear in ourselves the legacy of the sins of our ancestors; and, by virtue of the ontological unity of the human race, healing for us means healing for them, too. We are so interjoined that man does not save himself alone.

I found that the monks of the Holy Mountain understood this well. A monk is a man who has dedicated his life to God; who believes that if we want God to be wholly with us and in us, then we must give ourselves to Him completely, not partly. The monk renounces marriage and the fathering of children in order to observe and keep Christ's commandments as fully as possible. If a monk does not achieve his true purpose—to live his life on earth in the spirit enjoined by Christ—his monasticism has not been duly implemented. In other words, he neither assists in the continuation of the human race by procreating children, nor does he entirely further immortality through resurrection. He drops out of the historical plan by his refusal to take positive historical—not to say, political—action, yet he does not transfer existence to the spiritual, meta-historical plane. Having gained no victory on the universal plane of spiritual warfare, he is not helping his fellow-humans to attain the divine plane. However, though the monk may not realise Christian perfection, his striving, even so, helps the whole world.

O Holy Trinity, Father, Son and Spirit,
The only Truth and God;
Ever-living and all-powerful,
Who alone dost give strength to the troubled
and upholdest the weak;
O Thou without Whom the strong shall weary
and the firm grow feeble,
those who are full shall hunger
and young men shall bend:
Hear us in our affliction
and raise us to worthy service of Thee.
We beseech Thee, be swift to hear and have mercy.

When by the grace of the Holy Spirit it is given to a man to 'come . . . unto a perfect man, unto the measure of the stature of the fulness of Christ' (Eph. 4.13), such an event reflects in the most decided fashion not only on the destiny of all mankind—its influence reaches beyond the confines of history and reflects on the whole of cosmic life, for the world itself was created for man.

When we turn away from the path indicated by Christ—that is, from the deification of man by the power of the Holy Spirit—the whole point of man's coming into the world disappears.

9

Concerning Repentance and Spiritual Warfare

The whole of our earthly life, from birth to our last breath, in the end will look like one concise act. Its content and quality will be seen in a flash. Imagine a glass of the clearest crystal full of water. A glance will tell whether the water is clean or not. So will it be with us when we have crossed into another sphere. The most transitory reflex of heart or mind leaves its mark on the sum total of our life. Suppose that just once in the entire course of my existence I have a moment's wicked impulse, say, to murder. Unless I reject the idea from my heart in an act of contrition, it will remain with me, a black stain impossible to hide. 'For there is nothing covered, that shall not be revealed; neither hid, that shall not be known' (Luke 12.2). We often comfort ourselves with the thought that no one saw what we did or knows what we think. But when we look upon this life as a preparation for eternity; when we strive to get rid of the dark places within us, the picture changes.

'If we say that we have no sin, we deceive ourselves, and the truth is not in us. If we confess our sins, he is faithful and just to forgive us our sins, and to cleanse us from all unrighteousness' (1 John 1.8,9). When we repent, resolutely condemning ourselves before God and man, we are cleansed within. The water in the glass is purified, having been passed through the spiritual filter of repentance. So when I make my confession I convict myself of every evil because there is no sin in all the world of which I am not guilty, even if only for a second. Who can be quite certain that he is altogether free from the power of passionate thoughts? And if for a fleeting moment I have been held by an evil thought, where is the guarantee that this moment will not be transmuted into eternity? Therefore, in so far as we can see ourselves we must throughly confess our sins, lest we carry them with us after our death.

Straightforward resistance is not always the most successful way of trying to defeat wicked or simply idle thoughts. Often the best method is to stay our minds on the 'good pleasure of the Father's will' (cp. Eph. 1.5) for us. To conduct our lives fittingly, it is of cardinal importance to know that before the very creation of the world we were intended to be perfect. To belittle God's initial idea for us is not just mistaken: it is a sin. Because we do not see in ourselves, and still less in our fellow men, any permanent virtue, we behave towards each other like jungle beasts. O what a paradox is man—to contemplate him provokes both delighted wonder and consternation at his savage cruelty! The soul is constrained to pray for the world but her prayer will never fully achieve her purpose, since nothing and no one can deprive man of his freedom to give in to evil, to prefer darkness to light (*cf.* John 3.19).

Prayer offered to God in truth is imperishable. Now and then we may forget what we have prayed about but God preserves our prayer for ever. On the Day of Judgment all the good that we have done during our lives will stand at our side, to our glory. And vice versa: the bad, if unrepented, will condemn and cast us into outer darkness. Repentance can obliterate the effects of sin. By Divine power life may be restored in all its plenitude—not, however, by unilateral intervention on God's part but always and only in accord with us. God does nothing with man without man's co-operation.

God's participation in our individual life we call Providence. This Providence is not like heathen Fate: at certain crucial moments we do, indeed, decide for ourselves on one or other course. When we are faced with various possibilities our choice should be conditioned by the final aim that we have in view: the Kingdom of the Father. But too often we are influenced by other, more temporary considerations, and we turn aside from the true path offered to us by God, on to false tracks which will not lead to the hoped-for dawn. In any case, whatever we choose, suffering is inevitable. But when we opt for the way of God our sacrifice likens us to Christ. 'Father, if thou be willing, remove this cup from me: nevertheless not my will, but thine, be done' (Luke 22.42).

When it is given to man to know the overriding value of prayer as compared with any other activity, be it in the field of science, the arts, medicine or social or political work, it is not difficult to sacrifice material well-being for the sake of leisure to converse with God. It is a great privilege to be able to let one's mind dwell on the everlasting, which is above and beyond all the most splendid achievements of science, philosophy, the arts, and so on. At first the struggle to acquire this privilege may seem disproportionately hard; though in many cases known to me the pursuit of freedom for prayer became imperative.

Prayer affords an experience of spiritual liberty of which most people are ignorant. The first sign of emancipation is a disinclination to impose one's will on others. The second—an inner release from the hold of others on oneself. Mastery over the wish to dominate is an extremely important stage which is closely followed by dislike of constraining our brother. Man is made in the image of God, Who is humble but at the same time free. Therefore it is normal and natural that he should be after the likeness of His Creator—that he should recoil from exercising control over others while himself being free and independent by virtue of the presence of the Holy Spirit within him. Those who are possessed by the lust for power cloud the image of God in themselves. The light of true life departs, leaving a tormenting void, a distressing tedium. Life is bereft of meaning. When the Holy Spirit by its gentle presence in our soul enables us to master our passions we realise that to look down on others is contrary to the spirit of love. And if I have not charity everything else—even the gifts of prophecy, of understanding all mysteries, or of performing miracles—profits me nothing (cf. 1 Cor. 13.1–3).

Spiritual freedom is a sublime grace. Without it there is no salvation—salvation revealed to us as the deification of man, as the assimilation by man of the divine form of being.

It is essential that man of his own free will should determine himself for all eternity. The one true guide in the fight to fulfil this ineffably high calling is the commandment of Christ. All creation groans in the bondage of corruption, waiting for deliverance which will come through 'the manifestation of the sons of God' (cf. Rom. 8.19–23). It is sad to see that hardly anyone perceives what the genuine, divinely royal freedom of 'sons of God' consists in.

Intense prayer can so transport both heart and mind, in their urgent desire for the eternal, that the past fades into oblivion and there is no thought of any earthly future—the whole inner attention is concentrated on the one interest, to become worthy of God. It is a fact that the more urgent our quest for the infinite, the more slowly we seem to advance. The overwhelming contrast between our own nothingness and the inscrutable majesty of the God Whom we seek makes it impossible to judge with any certainty whether we are moving forward or sliding back. In his contemplation of the holiness and humility of God, man's spiritual understanding develops more quickly than does his ability to harmonise his conduct with God's word. Hence the impression that the distance separating him from God continually increases. The analogy is remote but this phenomenon is known to every genuine artist or scientist. Inspiration far outstrips the capacity to perform. It is normal for the artist to feel his objective slipping farther and farther from his grasp. And if it is thus in the field of art, it is still more so where knowledge of the unoriginate inapprehensible Divinity is concerned. Every artist knows the torment of trying to materialise his aesthetic vision. The soul of the man of prayer is often even more dreadfully racked. The dismay that invades him when he sees himself in the grip of base passions drives him ever deeper into the core of his being. This concentration within may take the form of a cramp whereby heart, mind and body are contracted together, like a tightly clenched fist. Prayer becomes a wordless cry, and regret for the distance separating him from God turns to acute grief. To behold oneself in the black pit of sin, cut off from the Holy of holies is distressing indeed.

Prayer often proceeds without words. If there are words they come slowly, with long pauses between. Our human word is the image of the Word that was 'in the beginning'. When words reflect intellectual knowledge they undoubtedly have metaphysical roots, especially where knowledge of God is involved. In this connection the fathers of the Church, in an endeavour to express the inexpressible in concepts and modes within the limits of our worldly experience, suggested a certain parallel between the God-the-Father and God-the-Word relationship and the correlation of our mind and our word. They distinguished between the inner, immanent word of our mind—the ἔμφυτος logos and the word pronounced, expressed—the ἐναρθρος logos. The former manifests a certain analogy with God-the-Word 'which is in the bosom of the Father' (John 1.18); the latter can be seen as an analogy of the incarnation. And if in His everlasting Being God-the-Word is consubstantial and equal with the Father, and reigning on a par with Him, in His incarnation as the Son of man He could say: 'My Father is greater than I' (John 14.28). Thus the human word uttered aloud conveys less than divine reality, knowledge of which was given in visions and revelations to the prophets, apostles and fathers. However, the vision when proclaimed was diminished more for the hearer than for the prophets themselves, since the revelation prompting the words was not lessened for them with their utterance. Just as for the Father the Incarnation did not diminish the Son.

Throughout the ages the doctors of the Church sought ways and means whereby to communicate to the world their knowledge concerning Divine Being. In their attempts they constantly found themselves torn between unwillingness to abandon their imageless contemplation of the essentially one and only mystery, and the love which impelled them to communicate the mystery to their brethren. God did, and does indeed, constrain His saints to tell of the gifts from on High. We see how this affected St Paul: 'For though I preach the gospel, I have nothing to glory of:

for necessity is laid upon me; yea, woe is unto me, if I preach not the gospel! For if I do this thing willingly, I have reward'—an effusion of grace—'but if against my will, a dispensation of the gospel is committed unto me' (1 Cor. 9.16,17). Thus it was with many ascetics through the centuries of Christian history. We note the same feature in Staretz Silouan, who writes: 'My soul doth love the Lord, and how may I hide this fire which warms my soul? How shall I hide the Lord's mercies in which my soul delights? How can I hold my peace, with my soul captive to God? How shall I be silent when my spirit is consumed day and night with love for Him?'

Impossible to keep silent; impossible to give voice. And this not only because words fail but also because the Divine Spirit inclines the mind to profound stillness, carrying one into another world. Again, blessed Staretz Silouan says: 'The Lord has given us the Holy Spirit, and we learned the song of the Lord and so we forget the earth for sweetness of the love of God . . .

'Merciful is the Lord!

'And the mind falls silent.'

10

Through Dark to Light

'A man is born into the world' (John 16.21). Before Christ no one ever greeted with such rapture the appearance of *man* as He Who had created man. The Creator of the universe rejoiced more over man than over the glorious choir of heavenly bodies. Man is more precious than all the rest of the cosmos. Man, completed and perfected, is wondrous, even as God is wondrous. He is immortal and supra-cosmic. He is more than a microcosm—he is a micro-theos. For the eternal Logos of the Father to be made flesh 'in the likeness of man' (Phil. 2.7) means that, with the gift of His love, man in turn may become like God, even to identity.

Between God and man there is and must be commensurability in spite of all that is non-commensurable. To dismiss this idea of commensurability would make it totally impossible to interpret any form of cognition as truth—that is, as corresponding to the reality of Primordial Being. If man by the nature of his spirit is not 'like unto God', then neither could God have been made man. In the lofty bliss of His all-perfect Being God, infinite goodness, desired to bestow this bliss 'outside' Himself, and so He created a world of reasonable beings. He did not create them for a part only of His bliss—any element of limitation would indicate unlikeness and rule out eternal unity with God on the highest plane.

The doctrine that man may become god-like, entirely, not just to a certain degree, lies at the root of our Christian anthropology. As the image and likeness of the Absolute, man is conscious that in his spirit he transcends every other form of natural being. In prayer we glimpse in ourselves divine infinity, not yet actualised but foreknown. Perfection of likeness, however, does not remove the ontological distance between God the *Creator* and man the *created*.

The tragedy of creation came with the fall, and continues in our perpetual instability. Prone to evil, we detest and fight evil; in our longing for the absolute good, for God, we push Him away and resist Him.

Christ, having linked God and man inseparably in Himself, is the one and only solution of the apparently insoluble conflict. He is in truth 'the Saviour of the world' (John 4.42). He is the measure of all things, divine and human. He is the sole way to the Father. He is the sun which illumines the universe. Only in His light can the way be seen.

We are naturally attracted to the All-Highest but our pilgrimage must start with a descent into the pit of hell. St Paul said of Christ: 'Now that he ascended, what is it but that he also descended first into the lower parts of the earth? He that descended is the same also that ascended up far above all heavens, that he might fill all things' (Eph. 4.9,10). And this is the way for us after the fall. In our consciousness we descend into hell, since the moment the image of Man eternal is revealed to us we become more sharply aware of our benighted state. We are overwhelmed with grief. The agony of our spirit is so acute that no physical pain can compare with this timeless suffering. With the last remnants of our strength we pray for help from on High. Brought low in sin, we see ourselves torn from God, and out of the depths we cry: 'Death has struck. Come and make me whole. Come and drive away all that defiles. Come and perform in me all that is pleasing in Thy sight. I am held captive, in darkness. I have no strength to rise to Thee.'

By darkness, by all that defiles, we mean pride. Pride is at the root of every sin. Christ began His preaching on earth by a call to repentance—to a radical alteration in our approach to life. Our normal perspective changes to its opposite: humility raises, pride casts down. God manifested Himself to us in absolute humility. This is the beginning of repentance which has no end on earth, for an end would indicate perfect deification—equality with Christ-God.

It is a fact that sorrowful prayer becomes all-enveloping. There is nothing left in mind or heart: death engulfs all creation, ourselves first and foremost. And, lo, there appears that which 'eye hath not seen, nor ear heard, neither has entered into the heart of man' (cf. 1 Cor. 2.9)—a ray of the uncreated Sun to pierce deep into our darkness.

This divine light, hidden, mysterious by nature, imparts new life to the soul. Immaterial and invisible, yet sometimes to be seen, it gently draws to itself the spirit of man; and the earth and its alarms are forgotten. Meek, it is more powerful than aught else. It comforts the soul; the heart melts; the mind is stilled. It is life suffused with love. Doubt and fear are driven out. Death flees before its face.

O Holy Spirit, mysterious Light;
O Light inscrutable, Light beyond all name:
Come and abide in us.
Deliver us from the darkness of ignorance;
and fill us with the stream of Thy knowledge.

This Light is the Light of Divinity. Ineffably tender, one is unaware of its approach. It may come in the night watch. Or at bright noon-day. As even light, entire, it is the breath of love. It brings peace. It brings an experience of resurrection. The spirit of man enters the realm where death is no more. Time is at a stand-still. The world, hitherto devoured by death, comes to life.

O Lord Jesus Christ, Light everlasting;
Who from the Father didst shine forth before all worlds;
Who didst open the eyes of the man that was born blind:
Do Thou open the eyes of our hearts;
and grant us to behold Thee, Our Creator and our God.

Grant us to perceive the Gospel word of Christ as undying Light, as creative divine strength, as a new step in creation; not now in the form of a command—'Let there be . . .'—but as a discourse with a reasonable being. 'Of his own will begat he us with the word of truth' (Jas. 1.18).

There is no vehemence in the word of Christ: man is free to reject, although the whole world will be judged by it. He who accepts knows from whence it came—knows whether it was pronounced of man or whether it did verily come down 'from the Father of lights' (Jas. 1.17).

Christ is the Light of the world. He revealed the Heavenly Father to us and showed us what man is. Without Him we should have little real knowledge of God or man. Christ is Eternal Truth transcending all 'scientific truths' which *per se* are ephemeral. It is impossible to know the Truth which is Christ otherwise than by listening to Him: 'If ye continue in my word, then are ye my disciples indeed; And ye shall know the truth, and the truth shall make you free . . . Verily, verily, I say unto you, If a man keep my saying, he shall never see death . . . If a man love me, he will keep my words: and my Father will love him, and we will come unto him, and make our abode with him' (John 8.31,32,51; 14.23). He will make us His abode, not for a while, but for all eternity.

Thus, those who in one way or another reject Christ do not know What and Whom they are rejecting. Christ is Wisdom, pre-eternal, hidden Wisdom which the rulers and servants of this globe do not know. ('We speak the wisdom of God in a mystery, even the hidden wisdom' (1 Cor. 2.7.)) Before Christ's coming the whole world, all the peoples of the earth, walked in darkness, ignorant of the way which leads to the Kingdom of God and our Father. Now these mysteries are revealed to us. To us has been given sure knowledge of the ultimate meaning of our coming into the world. Christ proclaimed the love of the Father for us, and in Himself showed us the Father. But we crucified him, and when He was hanging on the cross we mocked Him; and to this day continue to mock Him.

II

Experience of Eternity through Prayer

O Lord Jesus Christ, Son of the Living God:
We beseech and implore Thee,
Cast us not away from Thy presence,
and being not wroth with all our ungodliness
Appear unto us, O Light of the world,
to reveal unto us the mystery of the ways of Thy salvation,
that we may become sons and daughters of Thy light.

Stay your mind upon God, and the moment will come when
you feel the touch of the Eternal Spirit in your heart. This wondrous approach of God all-Holy lifts the spirit into the spheres
of uncreated Being and pierces the mind with a new vision of all
that is. Love streams like a light on all creation. Though the
physical heart feels this love, in kind it is spiritual—metaphysical.

In order that we may 'know the things that are freely given to
us' (1 Cor. 2.12) from on High, God withdraws for a while after
He has visited us. It is a strange sensation when God forsakes us.
In my young days I was a painter, and the natural ability has not
deserted me. I may be too tired to paint; inspiration may be
lacking; but I know that the gift is there, as an intrinsic part of
me. It is different with God. When God retires there is a void
inside me, and I cannot be sure whether He will return. He has
disappeared. I am left empty and dead. When He came to me, I
had something that surpassed imagination. And suddenly I am
back in my old condition which, before His coming, had seemed
normal and satisfactory. Now it appals me. I had been brought
into the palace of the Great King, only to be sent away. When I

was there I knew that I was kin in my Father's house; but now I stand pitifully outside.

These alternating states teach us how to distinguish between natural gifts and those which come as pure grace from on High. Prayer occasioned the first visiting. Again through prayer, but ever more ardent prayer, I hope for His return. And he does, indeed, return. Often—usually even—He varies the character of His coming, and thus I am continually enriched by further knowledge in the realm of the Spirit. Now there is suffering, now rejoicing—but I grow. I am learning to conduct myself in this new domain.

Of all ascetic practices the striving for prayer is the most arduous. Our spirit will be in constant flux. At times prayer flows like a strong current; at other times our heart will feel withered and dry. But the spells when we lose fervour should get briefer.

In prayer we are sensible of the presence of God which, though we do not achieve the plenitude of experience that we strive for, confirms our faith. We are nearing the end of our long search to discover the depth of Being—a search that in the past involved us in one spiritual adventure after another. Now we press on towards the goal shown us by Christ, not dismayed but inspired by the magnitude of the task before us. Our Creator knows better than we the ultimate potentialities of human nature. And if Revelation declares that we were chosen in Christ 'before the foundation of the world' (Eph. 1.4)—which John, Peter, Paul and other apostles, and the fathers, realised—how can we quail before the only calling worthy of heed, beside which all other aims and pursuits fade into insignificance? God bids each one of us to His feast but the choice—to accept or to refuse—depends on us. 'Many are called, but few are chosen' (Matt. 22.14). Of course, we are not more stalwart than the disciples who were afraid as they went with Christ towards Jerusalem; where He would 'be delivered unto the chief priests, and unto the scribes' (Matt. 10.32,33), and condemned to a shameful death.

O Lord Jesus Christ, Who art the brightness of the Father;
the express image of His Person;
the all-perfect tracing of His Essence and His Nature:

Open our hearts and stablish our minds that we may know
   Thee,
the only-begotten and beloved Son of the Father.
Behold, in fear and faith we stand before Thee,
resigning our despair to Thy deep mercy.
By the power of Thy spirit raise us to follow in Thy steps.

It is a strange phenomenon that with events of a purely earthly
character the word of a single bystander is often relied on even by
learned historians. But when the event is on another plane the
testimony of hundreds of witnesses fails to awaken the right
response. Why is this? I suggest that it is less because the testimony
is false and does not correspond to actual fact than because the
majority of us, satisfied with the things of the flesh, feel little
desire for higher knowledge. But 'flesh and blood cannot inherit
the kingdom of God; neither doth corruption inherit incorrup-
tion' (1 Cor. 15.50).

Eternal life was manifested unto us—eternal life 'which was
from the beginning, which we have heard, which we have seen
with our eyes, which our hands have handled' (1 John 1.1). Yet
in the twentieth century of New Testament history the world *en
masse* continues to live as though we were still in the Old Testament but without even vague expectations of a Messiah to come.
Worse, we do not even live up to the Mosaic Law. There is
suffering on all sides. The air resounds with the groaning of the
oppressed. Millions upon millions of unhappy people struggle,
if only for a while, to escape death treading on their heels. Day
after day we hear tell of starvation, violence, slaughter. The
nightmare has no end. Others may strain to find a way out of the
darkness of their spiritual ignorance: they hunger for Truth. But
when this Truth, apparently so sought after, so longed for,
appears in all its divine perfection, though 'the spirit indeed is
willing . . . the flesh is weak' (Matt. 26.41), and they close their
hearts to the power of immortality. Spurning Him Who said, 'I
am the truth' (John 14.6), they join the persecutors—and, as
Tertullian said, 'the best way of finding favour with the persecutors of truth is to dilute and corrupt it' (*Apologeticus* 46).

It is terrifying to think of people preferring anything in this world to the everlasting glory which the Son co-eternal with the Father offers us in Himself. Is it faint-heartedness that prevents us from believing in our high calling? Is our nature, which daily suffers corruption before our eyes, really capable of apprehending such sublime and holy eternity? Yes. He Who created us testifies to this. He took on the form of being which He Himself had created, in order, as man, to manifest to us in our flesh the perfection of the Father to which we, too, are called.

'Be of good cheer; I have overcome the world' (John 16.33). If He has so overcome the world, it means that as man He became supra-cosmic. And every one who believes in Him, by vanquishing the 'law of sin which is in our members' (Rom. 7.23) becomes like Him, supra-cosmic.

'Father, the words which thou gavest me . . . and the glory which thou hast given me, I have given unto them. Father, I will that they also, whom thou hast given me, be with me where I am; and that they may behold my glory which I had with thee before the world was' (cf. John 17.5,8,24).

To contemplate this glory we must needs be in this glory. Otherwise we cannot see it. To apprehend, even dimly, 'Who this is?' (cf. Matt. 21.10) we must become like Him by abiding in His word. Whoever has not followed after Him in faith; who has not loved Him and therefore has not observed His commandments, cannot pronounce judgment, since he possesses no grounds for forming an opinion. To appreciate the genius of a scientist or a painter one must be to a certain extent trained in the field of science or the arts. So it is in the sphere of the Spirit. Only when our life is founded upon the rock of His word do we receive an answer to the question, 'Who is this?' (cf. Matt. 7.24,25). Christ Himself said, 'No man knoweth the Son, but the Father; neither knoweth any man the Father, save the Son, and he to whomsoever the Son will reveal him' (Matt. 11.27).

Brought from nothingness into life, man is drawn by His Creator into the fulness of Divine life. God so loved man that He gives Himself to man without reserve. And in the same way as

84

God surpasses all that is in the world, so man when fully divinised by the Holy Spirit stands far above the world.

O Almighty God and our Father;
Fount of time and eternity;
Who by Thy power hast set a term to our life on earth,
and through Thine only-begotten Son dost grant unto us,
through resurrection, immortal life
and a kingdom that cannot be moved:
Accept us who implore Thee,
and sustain us by Thy Holy Spirit.

Man is indeed an enigma. The tragedy of our age and (more particularly, perhaps) the wholesale withdrawal from the Church and from Christ compel us to approach the problem boldly. St Paul wrote to the Corinthians: 'Howbeit we speak wisdom among them that are perfect: yet not the wisdom of this world . . . but we speak the wisdom of God in a mystery, even the hidden wisdom, which God ordained before the world unto our glory . . . God hath revealed them unto us by His Spirit: for the Spirit searcheth all things, yea, the deep things of God . . . Now we have received not the spirit of the world, but the spirit which is of God, that we might know the things that are freely given to us of God' (1 Cor. 2.6 *et seq.*). This is normal Christian understanding, without which we cannot 'walk worthy of the vocation wherewith we are called' (*cf.* Eph. 4.1). But, it may be objected, could not such temerity lead to pride? To counteract any tendency to conceit we have only to remember Christ's warning: 'And thou, Capernaum, which art exalted unto heaven, shalt be brought down to hell' (Matt. 11.23).

For a clearer picture of the Christian journey let us adopt the method resorted to by the fathers of the Church, and draw an analogy.

When we see a centuries-old tree with its branches reaching to the clouds, we know that its roots, deep in the earth, must be powerful enough to support the whole. If the roots did not go down into the bowels of the earth—perhaps as far down as the tree is high—and if they were not as strong and widespread as the part we see, they could not feed the tree. They could not support it—a slight wind and the tree would fall. We can observe something similar in the spiritual life of man. If, like the apostles, we recognise the greatness of our calling in Christ—that is, of our election in Him before the creation of the world to 'receive the adoption of sons' (Gal. 4.5), it makes us humble, not proud. This lowering, this humbling of ourselves is essential if we would preserve a genuinely Christian disposition. It is expressed in a constant awareness of our nothingness, as radical and all-round self-condemnation. And the deeper one goes in self-condemnation, the higher God raises one.

'Until now the kingdom of heaven suffereth violence, and the violent take it by force . . . He that hath ears to hear, let him hear' (Matt. 11.12,15).

12

Liturgical Prayer

Deep prayer comes gradually. Body and soul adapt slowly. It is particularly important for the priest who celebrates the Divine Liturgy to transmute his entire life into prayer if he would live this great sacrament to the full. Preparing himself in awe, and approaching with reverence, by the very content of his office the priest is drawn into the domain of the Divine. He begins the Liturgy by invoking the dread Name of the Holy Trinity, and continues in spirit poised between the Creator and all created being. He remembers the Last Supper; Christ's prayer in the garden of Gethsemane; Christ accused before Pilate; the cross and burial; the three days in the sepulchre; the Resurrection and Ascension; the sitting on the right hand of the Father—as the Son of Man now; and, finally, the glorious Second Coming. The priest likewise traces the creation of man, his fall and its tragic consequences; and God becoming incarnate in order to save the world. Mighty waves of cosmic life sweep through him. He will recall the needs and suffering of all mankind. In offering this holy sacrifice of love which requires total surrender of self, the priest opens wide his heart to embrace a multitude of lives and aeons of time. Thus he partakes in the world-redeeming sacrifice of Christ Himself; and in the act of communion craves not only to receive the body and blood of Christ but to apprehend His Divine life, also, in so far as may be granted to him by the Holy Spirit.

An intellectual grasp of the purport of the Sacrament is not enough. The priest's whole being—heart, mind, body—must unite in sorrowful prayer for the world. And the more he grieves, the mightier the healing power dispensed to the world through his prayer.

In essence there is no other Eucharist than the one that the Lord Himself performed. By his good pleasure the Eucharist, unique, is ever repeated; indivisible, it is constantly divided and shared, extending through time to the uttermost ends of the earth. The Upper Chamber grows, to contain the perpetual flow, gathering all people by the holy sacrament of communion into unity after the likeness of the Trinity.

'Holy Father,' prayed the Lord, 'keep through thine own name those whom thou hast given me, that they may be one, as we are . . . Neither pray I for these alone' [the disciples] 'but for them also which shall believe on me through their word; That they all may be one; as thou, Father, art in me, and I in thee, that they also may be one in us . . . And the glory which thou gavest me I have given them; that they may be one, even as we are one: I in them, and thou in me, that they may be made perfect in one; and that the world may know that thou hast sent me, and hast loved them, as thou hast loved me' (John 17.11,20–23).

According to the ancient theological tradition of the Eastern Orthodox Church, mankind is one being but multi-hypostatic, just as God is One Being in Three Persons.

The Liturgy in its eternal reality is the Lord's Passover permanently present with us. Before the coming of Christ the Jewish Passover commemorated the historical event of the crossing through the Red Sea—the moment when the children of Israel were saved from the Egyptian hosts. But our Passover is Christ, and He bade us commemorate in His Name: 'This do in remembrance of me' (Luke 22.19). Thus He, the true Centre of the universe (not some historical event) is the focus of our attention. This radically alters the character of the Easter festival. The whole Eucharist consists in 'remembrance'—understood not in the usual sense as a recalling to mind only but as an existential entering into Christ's world, into His Divine and human dimensions. Our Passover, and therefore also our Eucharist, is a passage from earth to heaven, from death in sin to the holy eternity of the Father.

Taking part as fully as possible in the Liturgical Act gradually teaches the faithful to participate in Christ's Gethsemane prayer. This is the pattern: when we are pierced by sorrow, pain, loss, we transfer our own hurt to the universal plane, and suffer not merely for ourselves but for all humanity. To the extent of our personal experience we can live everyman's tragic lot, his dread and despair. We call to remembrance the multitude of dead and dying. It may be that our suffering will at some point exceed our powers of endurance. Then, when mind and body can no longer keep up with the spirit, the spirit continues to follow after Christ, to crucifixion, to the grave, into the anguished hell of His love for mankind.

This noble science of the spirit is not acquired in a few short years of academic study: it demands our whole being. There is no end to this learning, since we never attain the fulness of Christ's love. By means of long ascetic struggle we gradually perceive the eternal meaning and especial character of His sufferings. We realise that they far exceeded, not only in quality but in spiritual strength, too, anything that the world knows. We do not measure up to Christ but all Christians must aspire to plenitude of knowledge of Him. To the extent of our perception of His redemptive sufferings, His eternal glory will repose on us. Through Him we become sons of the Father. Now we know that no man cometh unto the Father, but by Him (cf. John 14.6).

Such glory will not be given to us automatically, by virtue of Christ's merit, as many believe. Though all our efforts are as nothing compared with this gift from on High which is always pure gift, we must labour to receive and appreciate it worthily. Knowledge of Christ and of His Divine and human universality is a 'pearl of great price' (Matt. 13.46). 'And this is life eternal . . . to know . . . the only true God, and Jesus Christ' (John 17.3). It is 'that good part, which shall not be taken away' (Luke 10.42) from us by the death of the body.

Concerned that the faithful be rooted and grounded in true knowledge of the things disclosed by God, Paul the Apostle in fervent prayer 'bowed his knees unto the Father . . . that He would grant them, according to the riches of His glory . . . to comprehend with all saints what is the breadth, and length, and depth, and height' of the Divine providence for us which 'before the foundation of the world . . . predestinated us unto the adoption of children by Jesus Christ to himself' (*cf.* Eph. 3 and 1).

The same Spirit which inspired Paul to such prayer, to this day moves the hearts of priests and people to pray that every man may know with his whole self that God is our Father; that every soul may behold the Light of unoriginate Divine Being made manifest in the world.

The fulness of knowledge of the Most High God has not vanished from the face of the earth. The Church has preserved and from generation to generation hands on this knowledge and this spirit which are the quintessence of Sacred Tradition. The same Lord's Supper is celebrated day after day. The same prayer is offered up to God by His priests.

In the Eastern Church, before receiving the mysteries of the Body and Blood of Christ the faithful pray, 'Of Thy mystical supper, O Son of God, accept me this day as a partaker.' *This day* —NOW—speaks of divine eternity, in which there is no past, no future, but only the now. It is a prayer to be accepted into the divine plan.

Lord Jesus Christ, Everlasting King;
The one true High Priest;
Who didst offer Thyself to God the Father upon the cross
in atonement for the sins of the world;
and in this searchless act of service
didst give us Thine incorruptible Body for sacred food,
and Thy most precious Blood for life-giving drink:
Make us worthy of these ineffable mysteries,
that we may be partakers of the Divine Nature,
having escaped the corruption
that is in the world through lust.
We pray Thee, O Lord, hear and have mercy.

13

The Prayer of Gethsemane

Christ's prayer in the garden of Gethsemane is the noblest of all prayers by its virtue and power to atone for the sins of the world. Offered to the Eternal God the Father in a spirit of divine love, it continues to shine, a light that cannot be extinguished, for ever drawing to itself souls that have preserved their likeness to God. Christ included the whole human race in this prayer, from the first Adam to the last man to be born of woman. We lack existential knowledge of such love and so its permanent significance is hidden from us. Victorious in eternity, Christ's love on the earthly plane spells extreme suffering. No one has ever known such suffering as Christ endured. He descended into hell, into the most painful hell of all, the hell of love. This is a sphere of existence which can only be apprehended through spiritual love— how far we can penetrate the mystery depends on the measure of love that it has been granted to us to know from on High. It is vital to have experienced, if only once, the heavenly fire which Christ brought with Him; to know with our entire being what it is to be even a little like Christ.

'And being in an agony he prayed more earnestly: and his sweat was as it were great drops of blood falling down to the ground' (Luke 22.44). Let those who are ignorant of such love, and who have no desire to know, refrain from expressing opinions about Christ. Let no one venture in his folly to disparage the appearance among us of Christ the Immortal King, lest at the end bitter shame compel him to cry 'to the mountains and rocks, Fall on *me*, and hide *me* from the face of him that sitteth on the throne' (Rev. 6.16).

Though the emphasis does not lie on the physical suffering of

Christ crucified on the cross, the bodily pain makes the agony total in every respect. We know by experience that the soul can be more dreadfully wounded than the body. And if this is so with the soul in her earthly dimension, what must it be for the soul as spirit aspiring to eternity?

To know, if only 'through a glass, darkly' (1 Cor. 13.12) the way that Christ Himself travelled; to transform our physical nature into prayer at least palely reflecting His Gethsemane prayer during the most tragic night in the history of the world, we must accept tribulation. Adversity opens the heart to all the suffering in the world. The last stage of this great science of universal love comes when we arrive at the threshold of another life—when we are 'dying'. Many—especially in our day, are more or less unconscious during their last hours, and die without prayer. But it would be well if the Christian could cross over in a state of prayer, realising that he has arrived at the final judgment. Often we die little by little, and thanks to this gradual experience of death we become more and more able to assume the tragedy of human history and to apprehend the mystery of Gethsemane and, maybe, even of Golgotha.

In the person of the first Adam all mankind suffered a fearful catastrophe, an alienation which is the root of all alienations. The body was wounded, the skeleton smashed, the countenance—the image of God—distorted. Succeeding generations have added many another injury and broken bone to the wounds of the first created man. The whole human corpus is sick. Isaiah described it well: 'From the sole of the foot even unto the head there is no soundness in it; but wounds, and bruises, and putrifying sores: they have not been closed, neither bound up, neither mollified with ointment' (Is. 1.6). The slightest touch is torment. When people are physically ill they realise that others want to help and they put themselves gratefully in the doctor's hands; but when it comes to spiritual suffering they are resentful and ascribe their pain to outside interference. Thus with Christ: He, the one true physician, in His concern with the sores of our sin caused the most acute pain to all mankind. There is nothing more dreadful than Christ-Truth. The whole world fears Him. Is it not a fact that if we did indeed accept Christ's Absolute Truth, with our inborn longing for truth we could not refuse to follow Him? But a peculiar animal instinct of the flesh quickly tells us that to follow Him involves a readiness to be crucified for love of Him. Where and how shall we find the strength for such heroism? Christ's suffering is impossible to portray. In any case, no one would understand. Just as children do not realise the sacrifices their parents and teachers make to bring them up and pass on to them the hard-earned experience of a lifetime, so generally men did not understand Christ—and even the rare exception only partly understood. Thus the Word of Christ which calls for a radical altering of our whole life came as a cruel wound. When Christ beheld our distress He suffered more than any of us. And he bore this cross all the years of His service in the world. Golgotha was only the last act, the culminating point, as it were, uniting the whole: the mental distress of an infamous death, the wild vindictive laughter of those to whom He had caused offence, the physical pain of being crucified, the grief of His Spirit because men had spurned the tidings of the Father's love. He was condemned on all sides—by the Roman Empire in its zeal for legality and order; by the Church of the Old Testament founded on the Mosaic Law preserved from Mount Sinai; by the crowd who had received so much good at His hands. The disciples scattered. Christ was left alone, convicted and about to descend to those dwelling in the darkness of hell.

Christ is miracle beyond comprehension. He is the all-perfect revelation of God. He is also the all-perfect manifestation of man.

Every one of us will at some moment be brought to the invisible border between time and eternity. Arriving at this spiritual boundary-line, we shall have to determine our future in the world that lies before us, and decide either to be with Christ, in His likeness, or to depart from Him. Once the choice—to identify with Christ or to refuse Him—has been made, of our own free will, for all eternity, time will no longer function.

Until this moment of decision, however, while we are still in this life we shall often waver in our self-determining, hesitating whether to fulfil the commandments or give way to our passions. Gradually, as we struggle, the mystery of Christ will be revealed to us if we devote ourselves totally to obeying His precepts. The moment will come when heart and mind are so suffused by the vision of the infinite holiness and humility of the God-Christ that our whole being will rise in a surge of love for God. Overwhelmed by self-loathing for the evil in us, we hunger and thirst to become like God in holy humility, and in this longing lies the seed of holiness. Ever-growing love for Christ naturally leads to experiences that liken us to Him; and an unimaginable panorama will unfold before our eyes. The sorrows of the world will grieve us sorely. And we shall forget our body, and our spirit, in so far as it is able, will live Christ's prayer in Gethsemane. This is the beginning of the knowledge of Christ for the excellency of which St Paul counted all other things but loss. To win Christ and attain unto the resurrection of the dead, he was ready to reject all other gain. St Paul spoke thus, not because he had 'already attained' but because he was 'pressing toward the mark for the prize of the high calling of God in Christ Jesus' (cf. Phil. 3.7–14).

So, therefore, if the great apostle Paul had not 'already attained', neither may we make bold to set ourselves on a level with Christ. There must be a certain parallel, however. It is essential for all of us to bear at least a fractional likeness if we would call ourselves Christians. But St Paul aspired after a more perfect likeness and besought the Corinthians to emulate him (cf. 1 Cor. 4.16). Consequently, we must cast fear and faint-heartedness aside and in spirit follow after Christ that we may inherit life eternal in true knowledge of the Heavenly Father and of Christ, Whom He, the Father, sent into the world (cf. John 17.3).

It can be said with some foundation that almost nowhere is genuine Christianity preached. Christianity so far surpasses the ordinary understanding that the praying heart does not venture to preach the Gospel word. People seek Truth. They love Christ. But, in our day especially, they try to reduce Him to dimensions of their own making, which debases the Gospels to the level of moralistic doctrine. Yet Christ declared, 'Heaven and earth shall pass away: but my words shall not pass away' (Mark 13.31; Luke 21.33).

To attain to knowledge of Truth demands far more effort than it takes to acquire practical and scientific learning. Neither the reading of a vast number of books, nor familiarity with the history of Christianity, nor the study of different theological systems can bring us to our goal, unless we continuously and to our utmost cling to the commandments of Christ.

When, as I have said, a shadow of a likeness to the Gethsemane prayer is granted him, man then transcends the boundaries of his own individuality and enters into a new form of being—personal being in the likeness of Christ. By participating in the sufferings of His Divine love we, too, in spirit can experience a little of His death and of the power of His resurrection. 'For if we have been planted together in the likeness of his death' (in deep prayer for the world and consuming desire for the salvation of all) 'we shall be also in the likeness of his resurrection' (Rom. 6.5). When it is given to us from on High to enter this new sphere of Being, we arrive at 'the ends of the world' (1 Cor. 10.11) and pass into the light of Divine Eternity.

And every man on whom God has bestowed the rare and dread privilege of knowing to a minute degree the agony of Christ's prayer in the garden of Gethsemane will stumble on, slowly and painfully, to a cogent awareness of the resurrection of his own soul and a perception of Christ's undeniable, ineluctable victory. He will know 'that Christ being raised from the dead dieth no more; death hath no more dominion over him' (Rom. 6.9). And his spirit within him will whisper: My Lord and my God . . . Now, O Christ, by the gift of Thy love which passeth all understanding I, too, have crossed from death into life . . .

Now—I am.

PART II

The JESUS PRAYER

Among the many forms of prayer current in our day the Prayer
of the Name of Jesus has attracted widespread interest, and much
of what has been written on the subject is deserving of serious
attention. There have, however, been not a few absurd pronounce-
ments, and it would therefore seem called for now to devote a
separate section to the study of this spiritual exercise. The theory
of the Jesus Prayer can be set out in a few pages but its practical
application entails such difficulty that from earliest time the
fathers and teachers of the Church have constantly warned seekers
after this way of union with God to be cautious, to approach with
awe and to look for a guide already experienced in this ascetic
feat. It is not my aim here to examine all aspects of so exception-
ally complex a matter but to pass on some of the teaching given to
me on the Holy Mountain, first in the monastery, then in the
'desert'.

In the last hours of His life with us the Lord said: 'Hitherto have
ye asked nothing in my name: ask, and ye shall receive, that your
joy may be full . . . Verily, verily, I say unto you, Whatsoever ye
shall ask the Father in my name, he will give it you' (John
16.24,23). These words of Christ are the bedrock of the prayer of
His Name; and there can be no doubt that the disciples observed
this bidding—a fact which is all the more credible since they had
already learned the power of His Name. 'And the seventy re-
turned again with joy, saying, Lord, even the devils are subject
unto us through thy name' (Luke 10.17). Thus the history of
prayer in the Name of Jesus begins with the apostles who obeyed
Christ's injunction. There are no records of the actual words that

they used when they prayed in His Name but that they performed startling miracles—driving out evil spirits and healing sick people beyond the aid of physicians—is confirmed over and over again in the writings of the New Testament.

But what does God's Name mean? In order to pray 'in His Name' is it necessary to understand its significance, its attributes, its nature? Yes; not only necessary but essential, if our joy is to be full. To assimilate the inexhaustible depths of life in Christ requires our whole strength, the unremitting effort of a lifetime. The content or meaning of the Name of God is imparted to us only gradually. The fleeting invocation of His Name may rejoice the soul; and this is precious. But we must not halt half-way. Our earthly life is brief. We must use every hour of it to advance our knowledge of God. And when within us the bliss in our heart is combined with the light of intelligence, then, and only then, do we approach perfection.

I met with such ideas as these on the Holy Mountain. And naturally I wanted to learn from the fathers how they understood this aspect of the ascetic life. I arrived on Mount Athos in 1925. Not long before, stormy disputes had erupted concerning the Nature of the Name of God, similar to the controversy in the fourteenth century respecting the Nature of the Light that the three disciples beheld on the high mountain of Tabor. These conflicts have something in common with the secular clashes between nominalists and realists, rationalists and idealists. Sometimes the quarrel dies down, only to flare up again later in another form. We observe the presence of two distinct natural dispositions: there is, on the one hand, the prophet and the poet, with, on the other, the scientist and the technocrat. We will not turn aside to look for scholastic definitions but concentrate on the convictions that upheld the ascetics, the lovers of mental prayer, on Mount Athos in my time. In its theological aspect the problem is so vast that any comprehensive investigation is out of the question here. Let us, then, scrutinise the essence of the matter, that we may apprehend the imperishable knowledge that comes from on High.

Our individual lives are intimately bound up with our conceptions of the world and of God. And our prayer, especially in its ultimate degrees, demands the closest possible knowledge of the true nature of Being. 'Beloved, now are we the sons of God, [but] it doth not yet appear what we shall be. We know that, when he shall appear [in full] we shall be like him; for we shall see him as he is' (1 John 3.2). And likewise we also know that our mind *per se* cannot go beyond a postulate, cannot achieve the knowledge sought after. God must manifest Himself to man. Just as in the lives of each of us God presents Himself little by little, so in the history of mankind, as portrayed in the Bible, God gradually reveals Himself in various ways.

The first reference to invocation of the Name of God is not very explicit: 'And to Seth . . . there was born a son; and he called his name Enos: then began men to call upon the name of the Lord' (Gen. 4.26). Next, God revealed Himself to Abraham, Isaac and Jacob, on an ever-widening horizon: 'And I appeared unto Abraham, unto Isaac, and unto Jacob, by the name of God Almighty, but by my name JEHOVAH was I not known unto them' (Exos. 6.3). God termed Himself the God of Abraham, then of Abraham and Isaac, and later still the God of Abraham, Isaac and Jacob. To Moses God revealed Himself as a Personal, Hypostatic God: 'I AM THAT I AM' (Exos. 3.14). Later, God adds to His revelation of Himself: 'And the Lord descended in the cloud, and stood with him [Moses] there, and proclaimed the name of the Lord. And the Lord passed by before him, and proclaimed, The Lord, The Lord God, merciful and gracious, long-suffering and abundant in goodness and truth, Keeping mercy for thousands, forgiving iniquity and transgression and sin, and that will by no means clear the guilty; visiting the iniquity of the fathers upon the children, and upon the children's children, unto the third and to the fourth generation' (Exos. 34.5–7). Thus at first God revealed Himself to Moses as the one true I AM, with attributes still unknown. The subsequent revelation disclosed the properties of this I AM—God gracious and merciful . . . forgiving but also punishing. But this, too, was vague and Moses recognised that the knowledge given to him was incomplete.

Nor did the prophets achieve plenitude of knowledge. But from the words of Isaiah: 'Thus saith the Lord the King of Israel, and his redeemer the Lord of hosts; I am the first, and I am the last; and beside me there is no God' we see that the spirit of Israel was concerned with Primordial Being, with Him Who was 'from the beginning' (Is. 41.4). This God, 'the First and the Last', revealed Himself as Absolute, but Personal, Living: not some abstract, trans-Personal 'All-unity' and the like.

From the Bible story it is plain that every new revelation was accepted as a manifestation of God, as His immediate action. Consequently, the very Names signified the presence of God. The Name functioned in a twofold manner, affording both awareness of the Living God and knowledge of Him. Hence the dread of 'taking the name of the Lord in vain' (Exos. 20.7). As revelation of the Divine attributes richened so did knowledge of God in general become more profound and abundant. But despite the Israelites' persuasion that they were the chosen people, that the Most High God revealed Himself to them, until the coming of Christ the prophets never ceased to groan and their continual prayer was that God would appear on earth and bring the truly complete knowledge of Himself for which mankind naturally longs.

God manifested Himself as Providence, Saviour and much more besides but still remained veiled, as it were, in people's minds. Jacob, in the tragic moment of his life when he was leaving Laban to return to the land of his fathers, where his brother Esau still lived and whom he feared, at night, left alone outside the camp, wrestled with God (*cf.* Gen. 32.24). The years with Laban had not been easy; Jacob was afraid and distressed at the thought of meeting Esau. He besought God's blessing; though ready, perhaps, to argue with God, to accuse Him.

The same struggles occur in the lives of the prophets Elijah and Jonah. Elijah prayed: 'It is enough; now, O Lord, take away my life; for I am not better than my fathers . . . I have been very jealous for the Lord God of hosts: for the children of Israel have forsaken thy covenant, thrown down thine altars and slain thy prophets with the sword; and I, even I only, am left; and they seek my life, to take it away' (1 Kings 19.4,10). And Jonah cried, Lord, Thou didst command me with such insistency to preach to the Ninevites and proclaim the destruction of their city because of their wickedness, though I knew that Thou wouldst not do this thing for 'Thou art a gracious God, and merciful, slow to anger, and of great kindness, and repentest thee of the evil. Therefore now'—now that my prophecy has not come true and I am dishonoured—'take, I beseech thee, my life from me; for it is better for me to die than to live' (Jonah 4.2,3 [*cf.* Exos. 34.6]). Even more striking is Job's lamentation: 'Let the day perish wherein I was born, and the night in which it was said, There is a man child conceived . . . Let the darkness and the shadow of death stain it . . . let the blackness of the day terrify it . . . Lo, let that night be solitary, let no joyful voice come therein. Let them curse it that curse the day . . . Let it look for light, but have none; neither let it see the dawning of the day; Because it shut not up the doors of my mother's womb, nor hid sorrow from mine eyes. Why died I not from the womb? why did I not give up the ghost when I came out of the belly? Why did the knees prevent me? or why the breasts that I should suck? For now should I have lain still and been quiet' (in the vast quiet of non-being). 'There the wicked cease from troubling . . . The small and great are there' (in their nothingness) 'and the servant is free from his master. Wherefore is light given to him that is in misery; and life unto the bitter in soul; Which long for death, but it cometh not . . . Which rejoice exceedingly, and are glad, when they can find the grave? *Why is light given to a man* whose way' (to knowledge of God) 'is hid, and whom God hath hedged in?' (*cf.* Job 3).

Our destiny has something in common with all of these prophets. Israel fought with God, and which of us does not fight? Right up to the present day the entire world is in conflict with Him. All mankind blames Him for our sufferings. Life is not a simple matter. Yet to live without such knowledge is woefully tedious. Man hungers for direct dialogue with Him Who summoned us from the quiet of non-being into this meaningless tragi-comedy.

The main concern for each of us is to find out where the wrong lies—is it in ourselves or in Him, the Creator? It seems to us that we came into this world, not through our own will, and possibly without our consent. Do any of us remember being asked whether we wanted to be born into this life, it having been revealed to us beforehand what life would be like? Was it open to us to refuse the gift of life? Are we right to charge God with foolishness? (*cf.* Job 1.22.)

If there is no such thing as eternal life, then why the urge implanted in us to seek it? What is the meaning of our appearance in the world? Is it only to forget everything eventually? When will this loathsome spectacle come to an end? Are we being mocked?

Yet may it not be worth responding to Christ's call to seek the Kingdom of Love in the manner that He Himself indicated? If we are unable to create anything whatever from 'nothing', then the very notion of eternity could not occur in our consciousness. Its presence in us would be *ontologically* impossible. In the material world many ideas which at one time would have been considered audacious in the extreme have been implemented before our eyes. Why not let ourselves be convinced that the idea of blessed immortality and eternal union with our Creator and Father is likewise feasible?

How radical the change when we decide to accept Christ's summons! Every instant of our lives becomes valuable. Both suffering and joy are linked in a miraculous way with this new ascetic effort. The ladder to heaven is set up before us. 'Thy name shall be called no more Jacob, but Israel: for as a prince hast thou power with God and with men, and hast prevailed.' [But ask not after my Name, for it is a wondrous Name and thou art not yet ready to apprehend it. And yet thou art blessed.] (Gen. 32.28,29.)

'And the sun rose upon him, and he halted upon his thigh' (Gen. 32.31). The way to perfect knowledge was not yet disclosed. But a pre-glimpse was given, to be developed in the consciousness of the prophets, who would utter many fiery words concerning the Pre-eternal Word of the Father Who would surely come—perfect light in which there is no darkness at all would shine upon us.

Conflict with God is a risky venture: it can lead to perdition;

but it can also render us capable of 'putting off the old man with his deeds' (Col. 3.9). And the question arises: may not the spiritual crisis that we know in the world today be a prelude to a tremendous renaissance? Because what is happening now in the souls of a few can occur in a multitude of souls—can turn into a mighty flood.

Our present condition in the fragment of history which is ours can and ought to be a period of assimilation of being in all its dimensions. Our very pain, in the light of this hope, is an unfolding before us of a majestic scene. 'Day unto day uttereth speech, and night unto night sheweth knowledge' (Ps. 19.2), if spent in prayer which attains the boundaries of the universe. 'His going forth is from the end of heaven, and his circuit unto the ends of it' (Ps. 19.6). Prayer warms and rejoices us. It is the channel through which we receive revelation from on High. 'Blessed be the Name of our God from this time forth and for ever more.'

The process of revelation concerning God as set forth in the Holy Scriptures to a considerable extent parallels our personal progress. We grow in knowledge as did our forefathers and fathers. We start with a conception of a Higher Being. Step by step, more and more of His attributes become known to the human spirit, until the revelation reaches the dread power of the I AM of Mount Sinai, and man's understanding, though still imperfect, goes deeper than that of Moses. (*cf.* Gen. 22.14.) The wide stream flows through the centuries, bearing new knowledge of the Divine.

He Who is beyond all Name in His Essence reveals Himself to the reasonable beings created by Him under a plurality of Names: Light, Life, Wisdom, Beauty, Goodness, Truth; Holy, Eternal, Omniscient, Almighty, Righteous, Hallowed; Saviour, Redeemer; and many another. In and through each of them God, the One and Indivisible, comes close to us. At the same time none of His Names allows us to know Him 'as He is'. But He continues to reveal Himself through Names.

Twenty centuries ago the incarnation of the Logos of the Father gave tangible form to the idea of God as Saviour. 'The people which sat in darkness saw a great light' (Matt. 4.16). A fresh era dawned.

The new Name, Jesus, Saviour (God-the-Saviour) to begin with discloses for us the meaning or purpose of God's coming in the flesh: 'for our salvation'. The taking by God of our mode of being shows that it is possible for us to become sons of God. Our status as sons indicates that the divine form of being may be communicated to us. 'In Him dwelleth all the fulness of the God-head bodily' (Col. 2.9). After the resurrection He sat 'on the right hand of the Father', as Son of man now.

'The glory which thou gavest me I have given them; that they may be one, even as we are one: I in them, and thou in me, that they may be made perfect in one; and that the world may know that thou hast sent me, and hast loved them, as thou hast loved me. Father, I will that they also, whom thou hast given me, be with me where I am; that they may behold my glory, which thou hast given me: for thou lovedst me before the foundation of the world . . . I have declared unto them thy name, and will declare it: that the love wherewith thou hast loved me may be in them, and I in them' (John 17.22–26).

Our mind is stilled in wonder before this mystery. The Eternal and Invisible has taken upon Himself the visible and inconstant form of the created. The Spirit, dwelling beyond all thought, has become flesh and made it possible for us to feel Him with our hands, to behold Him with our bodily eyes. He Who is without passion submitted Himself to suffering. Life without beginning is linked with dying.

We do not comprehend how all this can be but we do not rule out that He Who created our nature could include it in His own Hypostasis. He did not assume a new, other, human hypostasis: He continued in His eternal Hypostasis, uniting the Divine Nature with human nature. The perfection of the Father appeared to us in the flesh; the compatibility of God and man was displayed with phenomenal impact.

Through Christ we know the Holy Trinity: Father, Son and Holy Spirit. Under the Name Jehovah, I AM, Moses apprehended one Person. He saw Word and Spirit as energies of the One

Who is. To us it has been given to know that both the Logos and the Spirit are Hypostases of equal worth with the Father. God stays single in His Essence but plural in His Hypostases.

The Name I AM by virtue of God's unicity applies alike to the Trinity as a whole and to each Hypostasis separately. Like many other Names this, too, can and must be understood both as a common and as a proper Name. Just as the Name Lord applies to all three Persons and at the same time may serve as a Personal Name for each of the Three, so could the Name JESUS, interpreted as God the Saviour. But we use this Name exclusively as Christ's proper Name.

With the appearance of Christ we come into contact with God to such a degree as to preclude any further revelation. He lived among us, in the circumstances of our fall. He spoke with us in our language. He revealed to us all things concerning the relations between God and man. He brought salvation in an extraordinarily concrete form. His preaching began with the call: 'Repent: for the kingdom of heaven is at hand' (Matt. 4.17). In this homily we discern a continuation of His dialogue with Adam in Paradise (cf. Gen. 3.8–19).

Great is the Name I AM; great the Name of the Holy Trinity; great also the Name of Jesus whose content is inexhaustible. It belongs to Him to Whom all creation owes its existence—'All things were made by him; and without him was not any thing made that was made. In him was life; and the life was the light of men' (John 1.3,4). He was in the beginning—that is, He is the principle of the whole universe. 'Immeasurably great, the Name of the Son of God supports the whole world' (Pastor of Hermas, *Similitudes* IX, ch. 14). Within the Trinity He is turned towards the Father. In the act of creation the same Logos is turned towards man created in His likeness.

The Name Jesus as His proper Name is ontologically connected with Him. For us it is the bridge between ourselves and Him. It is the channel through which divine strength comes to us. Proceeding from the All-Holy, it is holy and we are sanctified by invoking it. With this Name and through this Name our prayer acquires a certain objective form or significance: it unites us with God. In it, in this Name, God is present, as in a vessel full of fragrance. Through it God becomes perceptibly immanent in the world. As a spiritual entity, it proceeds from the Essence of Divinity and is divine in itself. As Activity of God, the Name transcends cosmic energies. Emanating from the eternal Divine sphere, it is not an invention of the human mind, although man has devised a word for it. It is a priceless gift to us from on High, meta-cosmic in its supra-natural glory.

When we pray, conscious of all this, our prayer becomes a fearful and at the same time a triumphant act. Antiquity was commanded not to take the Name of God in vain. Now that all the Divine Names have been uncovered to us in their more profound meaning—impossible before the coming of Christ—we should tremble, like many of the ascetics among whom I had occasion to live, when we pronounce this Holy Name. A worthy calling upon this Name fills the whole being with the presence of God; carries the mind into other realms; imparts especial strength and new life. The Divine Light, of which it is not easy to speak, comes with this Name.

We know that not only the Name of Jesus but all the other Names, too, are disclosed to us by God, are bound up with Him. We have learned to experience this thanks to the only-begotten Son Who bade us ask all things by His Name, in His Name. We know that all the sacraments in our Church are accomplished by calling upon the Divine Names: first of all the Trinity, Father, Son and Holy Spirit. The whole of our divine worship is based on invocation of the Names of God. We do not ascribe magic power to words as such; but when they are uttered as a true confession of faith, and in a state of fear of God, reverence and love, we do, indeed, have God jointly with His Names.

Generations of priests have preserved this knowledge of the power of the Divine Name. They have performed the sacraments with a lively and profound sense of God's presence. To them has been revealed the Mystery of the Divine Liturgy. 'For he commanded, and they were created,' (Ps. 148.5) sang the Psalmist, and thus it is in the Liturgy: the Name of God is pronounced over the elements, and they become the Body and Blood of Christ.

Disregard of the ontological character of the Divine Names, together with absence of experience of them in prayer and in the divine offices, has emptied the life of many. For them prayer and the sacraments themselves lose their eternal reality. The Divine Liturgy becomes simply a form of psychological or mental 'remembering'. Not a few even go to the length of thinking that prayer is a waste of time—especially when prayer for the fulfilment of material needs remains unheeded. But the most important miracle to be sought for in prayer is the union of our whole being with God—'that good part, which shall not be taken away' (Luke 10.42) from us by death. Our attention should be focused on our resurrection in God as the ultimate meaning of our appearance in this world. Love towards Christ, filling the whole man, works a radical change in us. As God-Man Christ united in Himself God and man, and through Him we have access to the Father.

Those who love Christ and His Name delight in reading the Gospels and Holy Writ. The Divine Names, their content and the light that proceeds from them draw the spirit of man to themselves, and nought else attracts. The whole of Scripture from beginning to end is full of witness to God through His Name. Listen to Peter's triumphant proclamation: 'There is none other name under heaven given among men, whereby we must be saved' (Acts 4.12). Earlier he had declared, 'Silver and gold have I none; but such as I have give I thee: In the name of Jesus Christ of Nazareth rise up and walk' (Acts 3.6). On another occasion the apostles 'lifted up their voice to God with one accord, and said, Lord, thou art God, which hast made heaven, and earth, and the sea, and all that in them is (Acts 4.24) . . . Grant unto thy servants, that with all boldness they may speak thy word, By stretching forth thine hand to heal; and that signs and wonders may be done by the name of thy holy child Jesus.' And when they had prayed, we are told that 'the place was shaken where they were assembled together; and they were all filled with the Holy Ghost, and they spake the word of God with boldness (Acts 4.29–31) . . . and great grace was upon them all' (Acts 4.33).

The human spirit progresses slowly in the sphere of knowledge of God. Years pass before the majestic panorama of Being opens before us and we contemplate the created world, and appreciate 'the breath of life that God breathed into [man's] nostrils' (cf. Gen. 2.7). Man becomes the connecting principle between God and the rest of creation, since in him the created is united with the Uncreated. The Essence of Divine Being is not communicable to man. But divine life is given to him by divine action. The act of the deification of man is performed through uncreated grace. The revelation on Mount Tabor provides a graphic instance of the divine nature of energy. Out of the bright cloud which over-shadowed them the disciples heard the voice of the Father: 'This is my beloved Son' (Matt. 17.5). The light and the voice (both inexplicable) were 'divine'. It is essential that we should all of us learn to distinguish energies by their origin: inability to do so hampers spiritual progress.

There is nothing automatic or 'magic' about the Jesus Prayer. Unless we labour to keep His commandments, we call upon His Name in vain. He Himself declared: 'Many will say unto me in that day, Lord, Lord, have we not prophesied in thy name? and in thy name have cast out devils? and in thy name done many wonderful works? And then I will profess unto them, I never knew you: depart from me, ye that work iniquity' (Matt. 7.22,23).

Our fathers were naturally conscious of the *ontological* connection between the Name and the Named—between the Name and the Person of Christ. It is not enough to pronounce the sound of the human word, which alters with the language used. It is essential to love Him Whom we invoke.

For greater perfection it is likewise necessary to understand the content of the life of the Beloved God. When we love someone we like uttering the name of the beloved and never tire of repeating it. It is infinitely more so with the Name of God. When we love in human fashion our love grows because we perceive more and more grace in the face of our loved one. His likeness becomes ever more precious, and happiness makes us notice new traits all the time. Thus is it with the Name of Christ Jesus. Gradually, our interest captured, we uncover fresh aspects of Him through His Name; and are ourselves impregnated with the reality, the knowledge contained in His Name. And this knowledge is essential to eternal life, as He said: 'This is life eternal, that they might know thee the only true God, and Jesus Christ, whom thou hast sent' (John 17.3).

2

The JESUS PRAYER: Method

I propose to devote this chapter to setting out as briefly as possible the more important aspects of the Jesus Prayer and the common-sense views regarding this great culture of the heart that I met with on the Holy Mountain.

Year after year monks repeat the prayer with their lips, without trying by any artificial means to join mind and heart. Their attention is concentrated on harmonising their life with the commandments of Christ. According to ancient tradition mind unites with heart through Divine action when the monk continues in the ascetic feat of obedience and abstinence; when the mind, the heart and the very body of the 'old man' to a sufficient degree are freed from the dominion over them of sin; when the body becomes worthy to be 'the temple of the Holy Ghost' (*cf.* Rom. 6.11–14). However, both early and present-day teachers occasionally permit recourse to a technical method of bringing the mind down into the heart. To do this, the monk, having suitably settled his body, pronounces the prayer with his head inclined on his chest, breathing in at the words 'Lord Jesus Christ, (Son of God)' and breathing out to the words 'have mercy upon me (a sinner)'. During inhalation the attention at first follows the movement of the air breathed in as far as the upper part of the heart. In this manner concentration can soon be preserved without wandering, and the mind stands side by side with the heart, or even enters within it. This method eventually enables the mind to see, not the physical heart but that which is happening within it—the feelings that creep in and the mental images that approach from without. With this experience, the monk acquires the ability to feel his heart, and to continue with his attention centred in the heart without further recourse to any psychosomatic technique.

This procedure can assist the beginner to understand where his inner attention should be stayed during prayer and, as a rule, at all other times, too. Nevertheless, true prayer is not to be achieved thus. True prayer comes exclusively through faith and repentance accepted as the only foundation. The danger of psychotechnics is that not a few attribute too great significance to method *qua* method. In order to avoid such deformation the beginner should follow another practice which, though considerably slower, is incomparably better and more wholesome—to fix the attention on the Name of Christ and on the words of the prayer. When contrition for sin reaches a certain level the mind naturally heeds the heart.

The complete formula of the Jesus Prayer runs like this: *Lord, Jesus Christ, Son of God, have mercy upon me, a sinner*, and it is this set form that is recommended. In the first half of the prayer we profess Christ-God made flesh for our salvation. In the second we affirm our fallen state, our sinfulness, our redemption. The conjunction of dogmatic confession with repentance makes the content of the prayer more comprehensive.

It is possible to establish a certain sequence in the development of this prayer. First, it is a verbal matter: we say the prayer with our lips while trying to concentrate our attention on the Name and the words. Next, we no longer move our lips but pronounce the Name of Jesus Christ, and what follows after, in our minds, mentally. In the third stage mind and heart combine to act together: the attention of the mind is centred in the heart and the prayer said there. Fourthly, the prayer becomes self-propelling. This happens when the prayer is confirmed in the heart and, with no especial effort on our part, continues there, where the mind is concentrated. Finally, the prayer, so full of blessing, starts to act like a gentle flame within us, as inspiration from on High, rejoicing the heart with a sensation of divine love and delighting the mind in spiritual contemplation. This last state is sometimes accompanied by a vision of Light.

113

A gradual ascent into prayer is the most trustworthy. The beginner who would embark on the struggle is usually recommended to start with the first step, verbal prayer, until body, tongue, brain and heart assimilate it. The time that this takes varies. The more earnest the repentance, the shorter the road.

The practice of mental prayer may for a while be associated with the hesychastic method—in other words, it may take the form of rhythmic or a-rhythmic articulation of the prayer as described above, by breathing in during the first half and breathing out during the second part. This can be genuinely helpful if one does not lose sight of the fact that every invocation of the Name of Christ must be inseparably coupled with a consciousness of Christ Himself. The Name must not be detached from the Person of God, lest prayer be reduced to a technical exercise and so contravene the commandment, 'Thou shalt not take the name of the Lord thy God in vain' (Ex. 20.7; Deut. 5.11).

When the attention of the mind is fixed in the heart it is possible to control what happens in the heart, and the battle against the passions assumes a rational character. The enemy is recognised and can be driven off by the power of the Name of Christ. With this ascetic feat the heart becomes so highly sensitive, so discerning, that eventually when praying for anyone the heart can tell almost at once the state of the person prayed for. Thus the transition takes place from mental prayer to prayer of the mind-and-heart, which may be followed by the gift of prayer that proceeds of itself.

We try to stand before God with the whole of our being. Invocation of the Name of God the Saviour, uttered in the fear of God, together with a constant effort to live in accordance with the commandments, little by little leads to a blessed fusion of all our powers. We must never seek to hurry in our ascetic striving. It is essential to discard any idea of achieving the maximum in the shortest possible time. God does not force us but neither can we compel Him to anything whatsoever. Results obtained by artificial means do not last long and, more importantly, do not unite our spirit with the Spirit of the Living God.

In the atmosphere of the world today prayer requires superhuman courage. The whole ensemble of natural energies is in opposition. To hold on to prayer without distraction signals victory on every level of existence. The way is long and thorny but there comes a moment when a heavenly ray pierces the dark obscurity, to make an opening through which can be glimpsed the source of the eternal Divine Light. The Jesus Prayer assumes a meta-cosmic dimension. St John the Divine asserts that in the world to come our deification will achieve plenitude since 'we shall see Him as He is'. 'And every man that hath this hope in him purifieth himself, even as he is pure . . . Whosoever abideth in him sinneth not: whosoever sinneth hath not seen him, neither known him' (*cf.* 1 John 3.2,3,6). In order in Christ's Name to receive forgiveness of sins and the promise of the Father we must strive to dwell on His Name 'until *we* be endued with power from on high' (*cf.* Luke 24.49).

In advising against being carried away by artificial practices such as transcendental meditation I am but repeating the age-old message of the Church, as expressed by St Paul: 'Exercise thyself rather unto godliness. For bodily exercise profiteth little: but godliness is profitable unto all things, having promise of the life that now is, and of that which is to come. This is a faithful saying and worthy of all acceptation. For therefore we both labour and suffer reproach, because we trust in the living God, who is the Saviour of all men' (1 Tim. 4.7–10).

The way of the fathers requires firm faith and long patience, whereas our contemporaries want to seize every spiritual gift, including even direct contemplation of the Absolute God, by force and speedily, and will often draw a parallel between prayer in the Name of Jesus and yoga or transcendental meditation and the like. I must stress the danger of such errors—the danger of looking upon prayer as one of the simplest and easiest 'technical' means leading to immediate unity with God. It is imperative to draw a very definite line between the Jesus Prayer and every other ascetic theory. He is deluded who endeavours to divest himself mentally of all that is transitory and relative in order to cross some invisible threshold, to realise his eternal origin, his identity with the Source of all that exists; in order to return and merge with

Him, the Nameless trans-personal Absolute. Such exercises have enabled many to rise to supra-rational contemplation of being; to experience a certain mystical trepidation; to know the state of silence of the mind, when mind goes beyond the boundaries of time and space. In such-like states man may feel the peacefulness of being withdrawn from the continually changing phenomena of the visible world; may even have a certain experience of eternity. But the God of Truth, the Living God, is not in all this. It is man's own beauty, created in the image of God, that is contemplated and seen as Divinity, whereas he himself still continues within the confines of his creatureliness. This is a vastly important concern. The tragedy of the matter lies in the fact that man sees a mirage which, in his longing for eternal life, he mistakes for a genuine oasis. This impersonal form of ascetics leads finally to an assertion of divine principle in the very nature of man. Man is then drawn to the idea of self-deification—the cause of the original fall. The man who is blinded by the imaginary majesty of what he contemplates has in fact set his foot on the path to self-destruction. He has discarded the revelation of a Personal God. He finds the principle of the Person–Hypostasis a limiting one, unworthy of the Absolute. He tries to strip himself of like limitations and return to the state which he imagines has belonged to him since before his coming into this world. This movement into the depths of his own being is nothing else but attraction towards the non-being from which we were called by the will of the Creator.

The true Creator disclosed Himself to us as a Personal Absolute. The whole of our Christian life is based on knowledge of God, the First and the Last, Whose Name is I AM. Our prayer must always be personal, face to Face. He created us to be joined in His Divine Being, without destroying our personal character. It is this form of immortality that was promised to us by Christ. Like St Paul we would not 'be unclothed, but clothed upon, that mortality might be swallowed up of life'. For this did God create us and 'hath given unto us the earnest of the Spirit' (2 Cor. 5.4,5).

Personal immortality is achieved through victory over the world—a mighty task. The Lord said, 'Be of good cheer; I have overcome the world' (John 16.33), and we know that the victory was not an easy one. 'Beware of false prophets . . . Enter ye in at the strait gate: for wide is the gate, and broad is the way, that leadeth to destruction, and many there be which go in thereat: Because strait is the gate, and narrow is the way, which leadeth unto life, and few there be that find it' (Matt. 7.13–15).

Wherein lies destruction? In that people depart from the Living God.

To believe in Christ one must have either the simplicity of little children—'Except ye be converted and become as little children, ye shall not enter into the kingdom of heaven' (Matt. 18.3)—or else, like St Paul, be fools for Christ's sake. 'We are fools for Christ's sake . . . we are weak . . . we are despised . . . we are made as the filth of the world, and are the offscouring of all things unto this day' (1 Cor. 4.10,13). However, 'other foundation can no man lay than that is laid, which is Jesus Christ' (1 Cor. 3.11). 'Wherefore I beseech you, be ye followers of me' (1 Cor. 4.16). In the Christian experience cosmic consciousness comes from prayer like Christ's Gethsemane prayer, not as the result of abstract philosophical cogitations.

When the Very God—ὁ ὄντως *ων—reveals Himself in a vision of Uncreated Light, man naturally loses every desire to merge into a trans-personal Absolute. Knowledge which is imbued with life (as opposed to abstract knowledge) can in no wise be confined to the intellect: there must be a real union with the act of Being. This is achieved through love: 'Thou shalt love the Lord thy God with all thy heart . . . and with all thy mind' (Matt. 22.37). The commandment bids us love. Therefore love is not something given to us: it must be acquired by an effort made of our own free will. The injunction is addressed first to the heart as the spiritual centre of the individual. Mind is only one of the energies of the human I. Love begins in the heart, and the mind is confronted with a new interior event and contemplates Being in the Light of Divine love.

There is no ascetic feat more difficult, more painful, than the effort to draw close to God, Who is Love (cf. 1 John 4.8,16). Our inner climate varies almost from day to day: now we are troubled because we do not understand what is happening about us; now inspired by a new flash of knowledge. The Name Jesus speaks to us of the extreme manifestation of the Father's love for us (cf. John 3.16). In proportion as the image of Christ becomes ever more sacred to us, and His word is perceived as creative energy, so a marvellous peace floods the soul while a luminous aura envelops heart and head. Our attention may hold steady. Sometimes we continue thus, as if it were a perfectly normal state to be in, not recognising that it is a gift from on High. For the most part we only realise this union of mind with heart when it is interrupted.

In the Man Christ Jesus 'dwelleth all the fulness of the Godhead bodily' (Col. 2.9). In Him there is not only God but the whole human race. When we pronounce the Name Jesus Christ we place ourselves before the plenitude both of Divine Being and created being. We long to make His life our life; to have Him take His abode in us. In this lies the meaning of deification. But Adam's natural longing for deification at the very outset took a wrong turning which led to a terrible deviation. His spiritual vision was insufficiently established in Truth.

Our life can become holy in all respects only when true knowledge of its metaphysical basis is coupled with perfect love towards God and our fellow-men. When we firmly believe that we are the creation of God the Primordial Being, it will be obvious that there is no possible deification for us outside the Trinity. If we recognise that in its ontology all human nature is one, then for the sake of the unity of this nature we shall strive to make love for our neighbour part of our being.

Our most dire enemy is pride. Its power is immense. Pride saps our every aspiration, vitiates our every endeavour. Most of us fall prey to its insinuations. The proud man wants to dominate, to impose his own will on others; and so conflict arises between brethren. The pyramid of inequality is contrary to revelation concerning the Holy Trinity in Whom there is no greater, no lesser; where each Person possesses absolute plenitude of Divine Being.

The Kingdom of Christ is founded on the principle that whosoever would be first should be the servant of all (cf. Mark 9.35).

The man who humbles himself shall be raised up, and vice versa: he who exalts himself shall be brought low. In our struggle for prayer we shall cleanse our minds and hearts from any urge to prevail over our brother. Lust for power is death to the soul. People are lured by the grandeur of power but they forget that 'that which is highly esteemed among men is an abomination in the sight of God' (Matt. 16.15). Pride incites us to criticise, even scorn our weaker brethren; but the Lord warned us to 'take heed that we despise not one of these little ones' (*cf.* Matt. 18.10). If we give in to pride all our practice of the Jesus Prayer will be but profanation of His Name. 'He that saith he abideth in Him ought himself also to walk, even as He walked' (1 John 2.6). He who verily loves Christ will devote his whole strength to obeying His word. I stress this because it is our actual *method* for learning to pray. This, and not any psychosomatic technics, is the right way.

I have lingered on the dogmatic justification for the Jesus Prayer largely because in the last decade or so the practice of this prayer has been distorted into a so-called 'Christian yoga' and mistaken for 'transcendental meditation'. Every culture, not only every religious culture, is concerned with ascetic exercises. If a certain similarity either in their practice or their outward manifestations, or even their mystical formulation, can be discerned, that does not at all imply that they are alike fundamentally. Outwardly similar situations can be vastly different in inner content.

When we contemplate Divine wisdom in the beauty of the created world, we are at the same time attracted still more strongly by the imperishable beauty of Divine Being as revealed to us by Christ. The Gospel for us is Divine Self-Revelation. In our yearning to make the Gospel word the substance of our whole being we free ourselves by the power of God from the domination of passions. Jesus is the one and only Saviour in the true sense of the word. Christian prayer is effected by the constant invocation of His Name: *Lord Jesus Christ, Son of the Living God, have mercy upon us and upon Thy world.*

Though prayer in the Name of Jesus in its ultimate realisation unites man with Christ fully, the human hypostasis is not obliterated, is not lost in Divine Being like a drop of water in the ocean. 'I am the light of the world . . . I am the truth and the life' (John 8.12; 14.6). For the Christian—Being, Truth, Life are not 'what' but 'who'. Where there is no personal form of being, there is no living form either. Where in general there is no life, neither is there good or evil; light or darkness. 'Without *him* was not any thing made that was made. In *him* was life' (John 1.3).

When contemplation of Uncreated Light is allied to invocation of the Name of Christ, the significance of this Name as 'the kingdom of God come with power' (Mark 9.1) is made particularly clear, and the spirit of man hears the voice of the Father: 'This is my beloved Son' (Mark 9.7). Christ in Himself showed us the Father: 'he that hath seen me hath seen the Father' (John 14.9). Now we know the Father in the same measure as we have known the Son. 'I and my Father are one' (John 10.30). And the Father bears witness to His Son. We therefore pray, 'O Son of God, save us and Thy world.'

To acquire prayer is to acquire eternity. When the body lies dying, the cry 'Jesus Christ' becomes the garment of the soul; when the brain no longer functions and other prayers are difficult to remember, in the light of the divine knowledge that proceeds from the Name our spirit will rise into life incorruptible.

3

The JESUS PRAYER as the
Prayer for all Conditions of man

It takes a long time to grasp the significance, the essential implications, of Revelation. Tidings of the salvation of the world are to be found in the Name Jesus. In an effort to absorb as much as possible of this knowledge of God we instinctively look back to the fall of Adam, trying to fathom the cause of this pre-historic calamity. We visualise the grandiose procession of events that followed the creation of man. It is made clear that the fall of Adam was preceded by a catastrophe in the celestial domain. We feel the need to understand what happened. What constituted the fall? What are its fatal consequences for each and every one of us? By the same token we thirst to learn the truth about salvation. And when understanding dawns in both heart and mind, then all that we have discovered can be concentrated into the one Name: JESUS. To pray judiciously in this Name means invoking Him; means incorporating in this word *Jesus* the act of creation and, subsequently, the act of divine salvation. He is our Creator. He is likewise our Saviour. He is our unique Teacher (*cf.* Matt. 23.10). He is our only way to the Father. In Him absolute Truth is made manifest to us. Through Him we know also the Father and receive the gifts of the Holy Spirit. In Him alone we are made worthy to 'receive the adoption of sons' (Gal. 4,5).

However, we confine our prayer to this one short Name only in those exceptional hours when we are too overwrought for a longer prayer. On the whole, we must slow down mind and heart, and keep to the fuller, more traditional formula which includes confession of our sinfulness.

When the Jesus Prayer with all its theological content is so grafted on to our heart and mind, it can replace all other prayers. Thus, we may well be concerned with our own condition, and then we pray, 'Lord Jesus Christ, Son of God, have mercy upon me, a sinner.' On another occasion, it is those nearest and dearest to us who preoccupy our thoughts, and we cry, 'Lord Jesus Christ, Son of God, have mercy upon us.' (In praying for other people we do not speak of 'us sinners', since I may only confess that I myself am a sinner—it is for God alone to judge other people.) Perhaps we are troubled about events concerning our fellow citizens, our country, the world at large. And then we implore, 'Lord Jesus Christ, have mercy upon us and upon Thy whole world.'

There is not just the one set of words. Some prefer to say, 'Son of the *Living* God'; others leave out 'Son of God' altogether and shorten the petition to 'Lord Jesus Christ, have mercy upon me (a sinner).' Still others may just pray, 'Son of God, have mercy upon me.'

Prayer in the Name of Jesus gradually unites us with Him. At first we may not know 'Who this is' (*cf*. Matt. 21.10): we are simply aware of strength coming from Him. But further progress depends on an ever-growing recognition of our sinfulness. And when we become so overwhelmingly sensible of the distance separating us from God that all is pain and despair—then do we begin in earnest to call upon the Name of God, our Saviour. 'Jesus, save me.' The unanimous witness of our fathers throughout the centuries of Christian asceticism insists on the extreme importance of acknowledging ourselves as sinners. Without this recognition there is no truth in our prayer. 'If we say that we have no sin, we deceive ourselves, and the truth is not in us' (1 John 1.8).

God breathed His breath into man, and we feel drawn to Him. We are tormented by the longing to reach Him, to be united with Him for all eternity. He calls to us, waits for us with love. This thirst for God colours our whole life. And in this state shall we continue to our dying day.

Christ thirsted for us to know the Father. He called to us: 'If any man thirst, let him come unto me, and drink' (John 7.37). 'He that believeth on me shall never thirst' (John 6.35). 'Whosoever drinketh of the water that I shall give him shall never thirst; but the water that I shall give him shall be in him a well of water springing up into everlasting life' (John 4.14). 'No man cometh unto the Father, but by me' (John 14.6). And we, in our urge to come to the Father call upon the Name of His Son: *Lord Jesus Christ, Son of God, have mercy upon me, a sinner.*

When we utter the Name of Jesus Christ, appealing to Him to be joined with us, He Who is omnipresent hears us. We make living contact with Him. Christ as the pre-eternal Logos dwells inseparably with the Father. God the Father enters into communion with man through His Word, through Christ His Son.

For the practice of prayer to lead to the results of which our fathers and instructors speak with such rapture, it is essential to follow their teaching, which stipulates, firstly, complete faith in Christ as God and Saviour, and, secondly, recognition that we are in mortal danger. The humbler our opinion of ourselves, the more swiftly our prayer rises to God. So soon as we lose humility, each and every ascetic effort is nullified. If pride is active in us, or fault-finding, or unfriendliness, the Lord stands remote from us.

We come to God as the most wretched of sinners. We condemn ourselves in all things. We have thought for nothing—we seek nothing—but forgiveness and mercy. We sentence ourselves to hell. And this is our continuing state. We ask God to help us not to grieve the Holy Spirit by our passions; not to harm our brother-man. We do not look for any especial gifts from on High. With our utmost strength we try to grasp the true import of Christ's commandments and to live in accordance with them. We appeal to Him: *Lord Jesus Christ, Son of God, have mercy upon me, a sinner.* God hears this kind of prayer and hastens to our rescue. 'And it shall come to pass, that whosoever shall call on the name of the Lord shall be delivered' (Joel 2.32).

People who are struck by a terminal illness, cancer, for instance, live out their lives in acute stress; but those who perceive the presence in them of sin, separating them from God, linger under even greater strain. They do indeed regard themselves as 'worse than all men'. And then new energy surges within them, generating the prayer of repentance which can rise to such a pitch of intensity that the mind stops and no words come. Only the one cry, 'Save me. *Lord Jesus Christ, have mercy upon me, a sinner.*'

This tension provoked by aversion to sin must be preserved lest we settle down to live with sin. Sin is so insidious; present—though often unperceived by us—in almost every step that we take.

'Then opened he their understanding, that they might understand the scriptures, And said unto them, Thus it is written, and thus it behoved Christ to suffer, and to rise from the dead the third day: And that repentance and remission of sins should be preached *in his name* among all nations' (Luke 24.45–47). There is nothing more important in our life than knowledge of the true God and of the way to union with Him. We must understand what *His Name* means. If this Name discloses to us the mystery of the love of the Unoriginate Father, then we shall love the Name itself. It contains 'the fellowship of the mystery, which from the beginning of the world hath been hid in God, who created all things by Jesus Christ . . . (Eph. 3.9) According as he hath chosen us in him before the foundation of the world, that we should be holy and without blame before him in love: Having predestinated us unto the adoption of children by Jesus Christ to himself' (Eph. 1.4,5).

It is vital for all of us through long years of prayer so to transform our fallen nature that we may be hallowed by Truth revealed to us before we depart from this world. The immensity of our task strikes fear into the heart. Prolonged ascetic effort shows us that everything in the Gospel revelation pertains to another, higher plane. The Light of Divinity is reflected on the earthly level as the commandment to love our enemies and be perfect as our Father is perfect. How would it be possible for us to obey this commandment unless He Who gave us the commandment takes up His abode in us? Hence our cry: *Lord Jesus Christ, Son of God, have mercy upon me, a sinner.*

Often when we would pray the Jesus Prayer the mind is besieged by inopportune thoughts of every kind which distract the attention from the heart. Our prayer seems fruitless because the mind is not participating in the invocation of the Lord's Name and only our lips continue mechanically to repeat the words. But there is meaning in this influx of untimely thoughts: our prayer becomes as it were a shaft of light focused on the dark places of our inner life, revealing to us the passions or attachments occupying the soul. We learn what we have to fight against; we see the iniquities that sway us. And then we call all the more urgently on the Name of God, and our repentance is intensified. *Lord Jesus Christ, Son of God, have mercy upon me.*

After long years of ascetic striving to follow the commandments of Christ, in the act of prayer mind and heart unite and jointly live the revelation granted by God. Man's primeval innocence and integrity are restored. Love and knowledge merge into an ontological unity. At first, however, it is the sense of love that predominates. For the time being love is all-pervading and one feels no need of other knowledge. The sweetness of love draws the mind into the heart, to contemplate in wonder what happens there. Only later does the commandment to 'love God with all our heart, and with all our soul, *and with all our mind*' (cf. Mark 12.30) set the mind working in its natural fashion. This process, also, is a slow one. In proportion as the light of knowledge fills the mind, so it, too, is seized with love towards God. The synthesis of love firmly established in the heart with the light of mental cognition is considered by the fathers to be perfection. But we must never rest content, never forget the perpetual possibility of subtle attacks from Lucifer whose intellect possesses cosmic dimensions. Only those come to know the sublime gifts of God who have approached the heavenly flame in fear and trembling; who steadfastly preserve a humble opinion of themselves in their hearts; who keep a clear conscience not only before God but towards their neighbour, towards animals—even towards material things which are the product of men's labour. They will care for all creation.

Prayer offered in humility unites heart and mind, and even the body is aware of warmth and hallowed energy coming from the Name of Jesus. After a time—the duration of the interval differs with each of us—prayer may become our constant state, accompanying us in all that we do. Prayer will be with us when we talk, when we are silent. It will not leave us while we are at work— and many (or perhaps not many) are aware of prayer when they are asleep. When through this prayer the Divine presence becomes so strong that the mind is drawn to contemplation, the totality of what we experience inspires words akin to those in Holy Writ. The spirit will sing hymns like the prophets of old; will find new songs of praise. But so long as he dwells here on earth the wrestler for prayer will by self-condemnation preserve his heart in humility.

Lord Jesus Christ, Son of the Living God, have mercy upon me.

There are two kinds of humility: human and divine. The first finds expression in the ascetic's conviction, 'I am worse than all other men,' and lies at the root of our prayer-life in the Name of Christ. Without this humility the second kind, that of Christ and proper to God, will remain for ever out of reach. Of this divine humility Staretz Silouan writes:

'The Lord taught me to stay my mind in hell and not despair. And thus my soul humbles herself; but this is not yet true humility, which there are no words to describe. When the soul approaches the Lord she is afraid; but when she sees the Lord the beauty of His glory fills her with ineffable joy, and in the love of God and the sweetness of the Holy Spirit the earth is quite forgot. This is the paradise of the Lord: all will live in love and their Christ-like humility will make every man happy to see others in greater glory. The humility of Christ dwells in the lowly ones: they are glad to be the least of men. The Lord gave me understanding of this.'

Christ told us that 'whosoever shall exalt himself shall be abased; and he that shall humble himself shall be exalted' (Matt. 23.12).

In Christ-like love there is no false humility, no inferiority complex. It is holy, perfect. The Kingdom belongs to it. It is pure Light in which there is no darkness. It embraces all created beings in joy over their salvation. It is saddened by *anyone's* downfall. The presence in our heart of Christ-like humility lifts the spirit into the sphere of Uncreated Light, where there is no death. It is felt as God living within us. The Scriptures declare that God is love. We might say that God is humility.

The Jesus Prayer will incline us to find each human being unique, the one for whom Christ was crucified. Where there is great love the heart necessarily suffers and feels pity for every creature, in particular for man; but our inner peace remains secure, even when all is confusion in the world outside.

Lord Jesus Christ, Son of the Living God, have mercy upon us and upon Thy world.

Some people when they pray in the Name of Jesus Christ try to concentrate wholly on Him. Day and night they repulse every other thought. This manner of life is mainly possible only in seclusion. Detachment of the mind from all earthly images affords profound quiet to the soul. But despite all its merit this is not an end in itself. The Divine Spirit draws the heart to compassion for all creation, and then prayer becomes a 'royal priesthood' (1 Pet. 2.9). Love that is directed towards the world is inevitably subject to vicissitudes, constantly affected by the shifts in the surrounding scene. Liturgical prayer uses appropriate wording for its vision but in private prayer we may keep to the one formula: *Lord Jesus Christ, Son of God, have mercy upon us and upon Thy world.*

It has fallen to our lot to be born into the world in an appallingly disturbed period. We are not only passive spectators but to a certain extent participants in the mighty conflict between belief and unbelief, between hope and despair, between the dream of developing mankind into a single universal whole and the blind tendency towards dissolution into thousands of irreconcilable, national, racial, class or political ideologies. Christ manifested to us the divine majesty of man, son of God, and we withal are stifled by the spectacle of the dignity of man being sadistically mocked and trampled underfoot. Our most effective contribution to the victory of good is to pray for our enemies, for the whole world. We not only believe in—we know the power of true prayer. But we do not ignore the apocalyptic prophecy that Evil will be allowed to find its ultimate expression and so make an end to the history of this earth. Then will come the final crisis—the Last Judgment—which will happen on the borders of time, beyond which 'the angel sware . . . there should be time no longer' (Rev. 10.6).

Meanwhile, we must never cease to invoke the Son of God to have mercy upon us and upon His world.

Eternal life in the bosom of the Holy Trinity is the root-meaning of the New Testament summons. Our urgent need is to conquer sin which strikes death into our hearts. Not everyone by a long way responds entirely to the Divine appeal. But there have been not a few witnesses in the past, as there are in the present, to declare that hardly has the love of the Father and the Son and the Holy Spirit touched our hearts before all our difficulties and suffering appear quite insignificant compared with the opulence of the gift, and in an indemonstrable but very real fashion we realise that we have passed from death into divine eternity.

> Christ is risen from the dead.
> By His death He overcame death;
> And to us He has given eternal life.